SCOTTISH JOURNEY

SCOTTISH JOURNEY

Edwin Muir

MAINSTREAM
PUBLISHING

EDINBURGH AND LONDON

First published in 1935

This edition first published in 1979 by
MAINSTREAM PUBLISHING COMPANY (EDINBURGH) LTD
7 Albany Street
Edinburgh EH1 3UG

Reprinted 1996

ISBN 1 85158 841 8

A CIP catalogue record for this book is available from the British Library

Printed and bound in Great Britain by
Caledonian International Book Manufacturing Ltd, Scotland

CONTENTS

SCOTTISH JOURNEY

PREFACE TO THE 1979 EDITION

Edwin Muir's *Scottish Journey* has the clarity and impact of a brilliant photograph. As a traveller's account it belongs to a genre familiar in writing about Scotland for centuries, stretching at least as far back as Aeneas Silvius in the fifteenth century, and comprehending such masterpieces as the account of Dr Johnson and Boswell in the eighteenth century and of the Wordworths in the nineteenth. Like the best in this tradition, it is no mere sketch of the scenery and buildings. 'This book is the record of a journey,' Muir wrote, 'and my intention in beginning it was to give my impression of contemporary Scotland; not the romantic Scotland of the past nor the Scotland of the tourist, but the Scotland which presents itself to one who is not looking for anything in particular, and is willing to believe what his eyes and his ears tell him.'[1]

For writing of this kind, it has no rival in the interwar years except perhaps Louis Macniece's subtle account of the Hebrides in *I Crossed the Minch* (London, 1938). Yet there is no sign that Muir thought highly of his own book: he mentions it neither in his first autobiographical sketch, *The Story and the Fable* (London, 1940), nor in its expanded successor, *An Autobiography* (London, 1954). His wife, Willa, gives it only a passing mention in her memoirs of their life together, *Belonging* (London, 1968). It was not, in general, favourably reviewed at the time. Certainly the years 1933 to 1935 did not evoke happy memories for the Muirs. Their five-year-old son, Gavin, had been seriously injured in a traffic accident in 1933, and made only a slow and partial recovery, during which it became clear that his hearing had been permanently damaged. In January 1934, Edwin Muir's dearest friend, John Holms, had died unexpectedly under the anaesthetic during a minor operation. *Scottish Journey* arose out of a commission from Heinemann and Gollancz (J.B. Priestley had already written a companion *English Journey*), and Muir hoped the advance would pay for a recuperative holiday for his family in Orkney. He had come up from his home in Hampstead to attend a PEN conference in Edinburgh in June 1934: Marion Lochhead has memories of him slightly chaotically chairing a session of international writers from the moderator's chair in the Church of Scotland Assembly Halls. When it was over, he set out alone on his journey in an old 1921 Standard car loaned by the painter Stanley Cursiter, a former school-fellow who had become director of the Scottish National Gallery: he toured the country in a heatwave, driving with the helpless eccentricity that was to become famous to his friends and acquaintances. His wife and son went north by sea to

Orkney, where he joined them. The book itself was written early in 1935 in London, before August when the Muirs made an unhappy move to live in St Andrews, where they spent the remainder of the decade. Edwin Muir was forty-eight when *Scottish Journey* was published.[2]

Something of the Muirs' unsettled mood pervades the book like showery weather. Yet *Scottish Journey*, for all its 'I am a camera' intentions and the private depression of the author, is neither superficial nor merely despondent. It is in fact a very carefully structured look at Scotland by an outsider who was also an insider, by a man who had already as a teenager suffered deeply there, and who had thought long about the political, literary and economic problems of the country to which he was returning. To understand this it is necessary to know a little of the early life of the author himself.

* * *

Edwin Muir was born an Orcadian, with all the sense of propinquity and defined distance from Scotland that that implies. As he wrote to his brother-in-law in 1926:

I hope the Scottish Republic comes about: it would make Scotland worth living in . . . but I feel rather detached, as I've often told Grieve, because after all I'm not Scotch, I'm an Orkneyman, a good

Scandinavian, and my country is Norway, or
Denmark, or Iceland, or some place like that. But
this is nonsense, I'm afraid, though there's some
sense in it.[3]

His father was a tenant who farmed ninety-five acres
on the island of Wyre; his mother bore four sons and
two daughters, and Edwin, the youngest, was born in
1887. The society of his childhood had for him a
mythic quality; it was an Eden described in the
opening chapter of *The Story and the Fable*, a place
where man and animals lived in a harmonious
environment; 'the farmers did not know ambition,
nor the petty torments of ambition'. The Muirs were
not rich, and their father was not successful even in
his pastoral world: 'by the exactions of his landlord'
he was driven from a good farm to a bad, to a worse,
and when Edwin was fourteen he gave up the
unequal struggle and decided to move with the
family to seek their fortunes in Glasgow. The move
was traumatic:

I was born before the Industrial Revolution, and am
now about two hundred years old. But I have skipped
a hundred and fifty years of them. I was really born
in 1737, and till I was fourteen no time-accidents
happened to me. Then in 1751 I set out from
Orkney for Glasgow. When I arrived I found that it
was not 1751 but 1901, and that a hundred and fifty
years had been burned up in my two days' journey.[4]

All his life Orkney remains for him Paradise Lost, and Paradise unregainable. At the end of *Scottish Journey* he made what Willa called 'the apparently naive statement that Orkney represented the only desirable form of life that I found in all my journey'.[5] Unlike most communities in Scotland in 1934, Orkney was more prosperous than in the years immediately before the First World War, but Muir recognised that it was a lucky enclave, and its Arcadian world of small farmers could not be returned to either by Scotland as a whole or, at a more profound spiritual level, by himself in particular.

The Muir family moved, in the winter of 1901–2, to the industrial world of Glasgow, where they took a house in a respectable working-class petty bourgeois quarter in the south side of the city. Edwin Muir's reaction to the change was one of disbelief at the moral and physical ugliness of the environment, and at the way the respectable middle class chose to ignore it. 'They gave me,' he says in *Scottish Journey*, 'somewhat the same feeling as I would have if I were told that a handsome, groomed and curled, socially popular, top-hatted, frock-coated pillar of business and the Church lived in a lavatory.'[6] He began work as an office boy, and then a chain of disaster struck the family. Within a year of their arrival, his father died of a heart attack. The following year one brother came back from Edinburgh dying of consumption: in 1905 a second brother died of a brain tumour; and a few months later his mother also died. He was still only eighteen, numb with bereavement, his own health so uncertain that he found it difficult to hold down his job as clerk: the four remaining children went their own ways, and Edwin went to live in lodgings on his own.

From this slough of despond he emerged partly because he found a cause and companionship in socialism. It is important to realise that Edwin Muir's conversion to a new political faith was closely akin to a religious experience – it was initially a matter of the heart, not of the head, of instinct, not of intellect, though it gave him an intellectual entree into a new world. He found in the Glasgow ranks of the ILP and the Clarion Scouts warm people, enthusiasts, sensitive to the chaos around them like himself, yet spurred by a belief that it could somehow be altered. It is clear how much Muir owed at this stage in his life to the fellowship and mental stimulation of the ILP, yet curious how detached he was from the hotly fought causes and working-class personalities of Red Clydeside over the next twelve years. There is no reference in his writings to the struggles in the munitions factories during the First World War, to Tom Johnston, or *Forward*, or to John Maclean.

Despite his affirmation of fellow feeling for the workers, his sympathies gravitated towards middle-class socialists like A.R. Orage, for whose paper *The New Age* he was soon writing. He admired guild socialism but seems to have spent little time in the company of real shop stewards. He was excited by

Nietzsche rather than by Marx. Perhaps he remained too much of an Orcadian cast out of Eden, and too much of a clerk, to feel deeply at ease in the company of the proletariat of the West of Scotland. He was always an in-between person, a loner, a man of indefinable class position, and he lived in the interstices of Glasgow society with friends in the university and in the pubs, but perhaps more in the former than in the latter.

Nevertheless, these years produced from Muir's pen a short but unforgettable account of the horrors of industrial life, albeit written down some time after his departure from the country. For two years he took a job as bookkeeper in a bone factory at Greenock where truck-loads of rotting bones were parked outside the office and an Irishman was employed to shoot the gulls that ate the maggots that hung in festoons upon them – 'for the seagulls could gobble up half a hundredweight of maggots in no time, and as the bones had to be paid for by their original weight, and as the maggots were part of it, this meant a serious loss to the firm'. Only an extended quotation from this early piece can explain what memories of industrialism were part of his mental equipment when he surveyed Glasgow in *Scottish Journey* twenty years later.

He had been in the town for almost a year. He remembered his first morning at the factory. His heart sank as it had done when he found himself drawing nearer to the heart of that soft, sickening stench which he had sniffed as soon as he set foot in the town: a stench coaxingly suggesting corruption. Ten days before he had been interviewed by a washed, ruddy old man in a shining office in a town thirty miles away; nothing had been said then about dead animals' bones: he had simply been engaged as a bookkeeper at two pounds a week.

He remembered the first days spent in fighting down his disgust. There was a whiff of obscenity in the stench which rose from the bones when they burned in the furnace, and the thick, oily smoke hung about in stagnant coils. On thunder-laden days the smell stood solid in the air, stirring slightly, fanning his cheek as with the brush of soiled wings; at those times it seemed to be palpable, permeating his clothes and coating his skin, and when he reached his lodgings he had to strip and wash all over until he felt clean again. Sometimes he fancied that the smell always clung to him, that it had soaked into his skin and went about with him like a corrupt aura. He had heard that the men and women who worked in the yard, unloading the bones and casting them into the furnace, never got rid of the smell, no matter how they scrubbed. It got among the women's hair and into the pores of their skin. They breathed it into the faces of their lovers when at night, under the hawthorn bushes outside the town, they found a few moments' sensual forgetfulness; they breathed it out with their last breath, infecting the Host which the priest set between their lips, and making it taste of McClintock's bone factory. A thing so tenacious and so vile had given him at first a feeling of mystical revulsion; but he had got used to it; he was almost immune now with the immunity of habituation.[7]

Edwin Muir left Scotland for London in 1919, after his marriage to Willa Anderson. The Muirs had relatively little contact with Scotland between then and 1932, when Helen Cruikshank invited them north as part of the plan pursued by the Scottish branch of PEN International to tempt back into Scotland writers living outside. The following year they had a holiday in Orkney, and the idea for *Scottish Journey* came to Edwin Muir as he was driving that summer through the mining districts of Lanarkshire deeply stricken with unemployment. 'Airdrie and Motherwell are the most improbable places imaginable in which to be left with nothing to do; for only rough work could reconcile anyone to living in them.' It was to be a book about a second 'clearance' of Scotland, comparable to the Highland clearances of the nineteenth century, 'a silent clearance . . . a clearance not of human beings, but of what they depend upon for life'.[8] In 1934 he was making the journey and in 1935 writing the book.

The Scotland of the early 1930s was indeed a very different place from the Scotland Muir had known before the First World War. Edwardian Scotland, for all its brutality and squalor, was imbued with the confidence that comes with economic vitality. The Clyde in 1913 launched 750,000 tons of shipping, more than the total output of either Germany or the USA, and equivalent to 18 per cent of world production. Scotland manufactured about a fifth of the UK's steel output and 13.5 per cent of its pig-iron. It employed 140,000 coal-miners. In textiles, the jute industry of Dundee and the tweed mills of the Borders were in the full flood of prosperity. By 1933 the Clyde was launching merely 56,000 tons of shipping, and the extraordinarily high figure of 69 per cent of insured workers in the Scottish ship-building and ship repair trade were unemployed. Scotland now manufactured only 11.5 per cent of Britain's steel and 5.5 per cent of her pig-iron: and her output was respectively 56 per cent and 16 per cent of the 1913 figure. The coal industry was finding work for only 80,000 hands and producing a third less coal. The Dundee jute trade was deeply depressed and the Borders woollen industry for the greater part of the year was on part-time working. Nor could Scotland hope to make up on the rural roundabouts what she was losing on the urban swings: in the late 1920s the value of gross output of Scottish farming was falling while it was still rising in England, and in the fishing industry the numbers of those employed and the value of the catch were both steadily dropping. It is impossible to tell what the average rate of Scottish unemployment was before the First World War, but it cannot have been high except in some years of cyclical depression like 1907: in the 1920s it never fell below 10 per cent, and in 1933 stood at 26 per cent (with England then about 20 per cent). Average income per head in Scotland dropped from about 92 per cent of the UK average in the late 1920s to 86 per cent in 1933. Sapped by emigration to more favoured countries, even the population itself declined for the first (and only) time since the census began in 1801: in 1931 it was 40,000 less than it had been in 1921. Shetland in the decennial period lost 17 per cent of its population, Ross and Cromarty 12 per cent, Caithness 11.5 per cent; the four largest cities, on the other hand, gained 4 per cent, indicative of the feeling that while life might be difficult in the large towns it was not so hopeless of future prospects as the countryside.

The malaise of which all these downward-pointing economic indicators are symptoms was of considerable complexity. The high levels of unemployment that Scotland experienced throughout the 1920s were shared with the entire UK, and were part and parcel of the economic problems of Britain in that decade, of an economy hit by over-commitment to a handful of basic industries geared to a failing export trade and unable to adjust to the altered circumstances of the post-war world. The particular depths of the years 1929–33 were additionally the consequences of the Great Slump that commenced on Wall Street and spread over the western world, an unprecedented failure of demand and of confidence which made many profounder economic thinkers than Edwin Muir wonder whether the Armageddon of capitalism so long foretold by the Marxists was not now at hand. The slow recovery of Scotland from 1933 compared especially to the south of England points to the continuing weakness of the Scottish economy, with so high a proportion of its factors of production tied up in unsuccessful staple industries and so few involved in the new or successful ones of the Midlands or the London area, like cars, aircraft, chemicals, electrical goods, artificial fibres and non-ferrous metals.

This imbalance was increased by the lack of effective state regional policies and (in their absence) by the vigour of so-called 'rationalisation' policies that were carried out by combines of businessmen in the interwar years. As the *Survey of Economic Conditions in Scotland,* published for the first time by the Clydesdale Bank in February 1934, noted, the concentration of iron and steel production had tended to move the industry south, and 'the closing down of redundant shipyards has taken heavy toll on the Clyde': even such government actions as there had been had either ignored Scotland (e.g. by giving a guaranteed price to farmers for their wheat but not their oats) or had made the situation worse (the Greenock cane-sugar refining industry was ruined by state subsidies to beet-sugar production).

The economic upheavals in the country to which

Edwin Muir was returning were accompanied by party political changes which, as an old ILP campaigner, he could have been expected to welcome, at least down to 1931. The old safe Liberal country which had once provided Mr Gladstone with such loyal support was still alive on the eve of the First World War: in the general election of 1910, fifty-eight Liberals had been returned in Scotland, with eleven Tories and three members of the new Labour Party. Then it fell, and Labour rose. By 1918 there were seven Labour members, by 1922 thirty, by 1929 thirty-eight. The collapse of the second minority Labour government and the fracture of the party under Ramsay Macdonald in 1931 reduced Labour representation to seven, with all the other seats going to the Tory-led coalition. Nevertheless, Labour was far from done, especially at local level where politicians were relatively immune from the bad name given by party blunders at Westminster; in 1933 they captured control of Glasgow at the municipal elections, and in the general election of 1935 bounced back with twenty-four Labour and ILP members. This rise of the Left plainly gave hope to Muir, disillusioned and disappointed though he was by the behaviour of the Labour Party in office; similarly, the right-wing backlash of 1931 filled him with foreboding, not least for the future of the trade unions: 'if Capitalism manages finally to smash these unions', he says in a striking passage in *Scottish Journey*, 'it will be a loss to civilisation greater than the loss that would be brought about by another war'.[9]

Nevertheless, at least as interesting to Muir as the rise of Labour was the stirrings (as yet quite unrewarded by success at the polls) of Scottish Nationalism.[10] The National Party of Scotland had surfaced as a political organisation in 1928, to work for 'self-government for Scotland with independent national status within the British group of nations, together with the reconstruction of Scottish national life'. From the start it was closely associated with the literary figures of the Scottish Renaissance, and C.M. Grieve (Hugh MacDiarmid) was one of the four first prospective parliamentary candidates to be announced. In 1932 a separate and quite different Scottish Party arose as a result of a revolt in the Tory association at Cathcart. It declared itself in favour of 'Imperial Federation and Scottish Home Rule'. In 1934 the two amalgamated to form the Scottish National Party under John MacCormick, but only after purges in the National Party of Scotland had got rid of left-wing and literary wild men who opposed what they regarded as the watering-down of the Scottish independence movement.

Muir was both caught up in this nationalist movement and detached from it. He was still a friend of Grieve (with whom, however, he came to quarrel most bitterly in 1936 after Muir's attack in *Scott and Scotland* on the futility of Scottish writers attempting to communicate through a made-up Lallans). Muir was a prominent figure in the nationalist-led Scottish Centre of PEN International, and in 1932 at the International Congress at Budapest had successfully, and in the face of some unpleasantness, asserted Scotland's claim to separate national identity from the English Centre, which was endeavouring to claim it as a regional offshoot.[11] He embarked on his journey round Scotland fresh from the heady atmosphere of the Edinburgh PEN Congress which had tried to demonstrate to the world the reality and vigour of the Scottish Renaissance. On the other hand, Muir was a Hampstead-living Orcadian whose young political conversion and continuing friendship with A.R. Orage (until the latter's death in 1934) had drawn him in the direction of a variety of socialist and quasi-socialist ideas current in the south.

Of these the most beguiling at the time of *Scottish Journey* were the ideas of a fellow Scot, Major C.H. Douglas, whose 'social credit' theories had a curious attraction not only to Muir and Orage but to C.M. Grieve and even to Ezra Pound. Muir himself wrote an eloquent pamphlet in the same year as *Scottish Journey*, 'Social Credit and the Labour Party', which said little about the Douglas scheme but a good deal about his own views on the immorality of capitalism and the value of trying alternative paths to Socialism than that represented by Marx. Muir indeed had grave misgivings about Marxism, whose ideas of the class war he found distasteful and barren, explaining nothing but themselves. On the other hand, only the poets' own lack of knowledge of elementary economics could have allowed them to take Major Douglas's theories (which even G.D.H. Cole characterised as a 'piece of nonsense') so seriously.[12] Douglas proposed a programme of 'new economics' in order to revive consumer demand and make a peaceful transition to a new economic order possible. All credit should be nationalised; a national dividend based on the computed value of all the capital assets in the country should be issued to every family (he expected it to amount to over £300 per household in Scotland in the first year);[13] wages should be reduced by up to 25 per cent to help pay for it; the free market should be replaced by administered prices and by a state profit-sharing system not unlike the co-op's divvy. Finally, Douglas would have reduced the hours worked by any one person in government offices to four a day, while doubling the number of existing civil servants, the second shift being intended to check on the first. That Muir and others should feel the pull of such a farrago of confusion may perhaps be explained by their reluctance to accept either the kind of labourism perpetuating the capitalist system represented by Ramsay Macdonald, or the ruthless bureaucratic state communism represented by Soviet Russia, which seemed the main alternative. It is as good an illustration as any of the fact that Muir's socialism was of the heart rather than the head.

* * *

Scottish Journey, then, was written against this personal, economic and political background. For all its wit and sharpness of surface observation, it is very seriously concerned about identity, the economic order and the political plight of Scotland, in a way that none of Edwin Muir's other writings were. Of the three, however, it is plainly the search for Scottish identity that takes primacy in Muir's mind. The elusive nature of this quarry and the subtle character of the search gives the book its lasting significance.

It begins in Edinburgh, and if there had been no more to *Scottish Journey* than its opening chapter it would still have won a place among the immortal pieces of Scottish descriptive writing. It is an account of the tea-shops 'more strange than a dream', where ladies and clerks sit in an atmosphere of subdued eroticism among the sad decor and the pale music; of pubs from which women are excluded but where men 'wrapped in a safe cloak of alcohol' behave 'like a company of souls reborn by Freud'; of pedestrians who love to parade the streets before one another: 'nowhere that I have been is one so bathed and steeped and rolled about in floating sexual desire as in certain streets of Glasgow and Edinburgh'. But its theme is of a city, split physically between Old Town and New, but also socially and spiritually between the poor and rich, the poor who have the Old Town and the rich the New, with only the prostitutes who dare to walk in comfort in both: 'a wholesale invasion of

Princes Street by the poor would be felt not only as an offence against good taste but as a blasphemy'.

The origins and character of this split, implies Muir, have to do with the class nature of modern life, for there is little left that is specifically Scottish about Edinburgh or the Edinburgh people. Such as there once was has been levelled by 'the film, the press, the radio, the lending library, or the public schools'. So do not seek your Scottish Scotland here, he implies, and sets off south in his car.

The next two chapters have to do with small-town life in the Borders and Ayrshire, showing some spirit and independence in the Tweed towns but little but lassitude in the west. The Scottish identity here is mean, as miserable as the 'insect life' lived by Sir James Barrie's characters in *A Window in Thrums*, a 'dead silence punctuated by malicious whispers and hiccups'. In Ayrshire he visits a village where for a time as a young man he found a job as an apprentice chauffeur, but its old rough 'acrimonious vigour' had been crushed by a decade of unemployment and emigration. There is not much in the little towns, he seems to say, that contains enough energy to drag Scotland out of its plight.

These chapters also give Muir the opportunity to visit Abbotsford and Ayr, and to tilt at the cults and reputations of Sir Walter Scott and Robert Burns – 'sham bards of a sham nation', he called them elsewhere.[14] For so good a literary critic, the judgements seem as remarkably superficial as they are stinging:

it is neither helpful nor true to describe 'Annie Laurie' as 'a unique anthology of hackneyed similes'. But the point is not to write an essay in serious criticism but to mock the idols of the tea-rooms and the church socials, and to attack the forefathers of the 'kailyard' school of romantic popular literature whose effusions blinded Scotland to the possibility of seeing itself as it really was. Attacks like these, like the attacks on John Knox and the Presbyterian Church in which Muir also engaged with much fury, were not unique among the *litterati* of the Scottish Renaissance; Catherine and Donald Carsewell and George Scott Moncrieff, for example, engaged on similar demolition jobs.[15] Of all the identities the inhabitants of Scotland might assume, the falsest of all, implies Muir, is the mark of couthy sentimentality and religiosity.

And so he arrives in Glasgow, the scene of his personal traumas and the enormous heart of modern Scotland. But it is a rotting heart – morally, it has been rotting for a century through its toleration of greed, poverty and slums; economically, it is rotting in the depression that has silenced the shipyards and the factories and emptied the workforce on to the sunny streets where they acquire unnatural tans. This is another piece of excellent sustained writing, and again the serious message is that there is nothing specifically Scottish about the character of the city: it is the misbegotten child of an industrial capitalism itself so monstrous as to be incurable by any purely Scottish surgery. The only people of real humanity in the city are the socialists, because they alone dare to look upon the slums and to imagine and work towards a world where they and the system that created them could be destroyed. Everyone else attempts to distance themselves from the facts of exploitation and squalor by the private cultivation of greed and a guilty respectability. This writing is very political, if not very specific about the precise nature of solutions; it is more negative than positive, and says that the Scottish identity here, if there is one, is overwhelmed by the 'total volume of colourless or bug-coloured poverty'. Furthermore, the industrial world that made the city what it was is now visibly falling – what can you do with an industrial city without industry, for you plainly cannot return to pre-industrial history?

The remainder of the book winds away from Glasgow back into the rural world. His journey through Lanarkshire, where he could have been expected to dwell on the plight of the mining villages (especially as the sight of their unemployed the previous year had given him the idea for the book) is diverted to a Catholic grotto at Carfin, which he describes at great length. The oddness of this passage – for he was genuinely moved by the devotion of the priest and workers who had created it in the midst of a howling industrial wilderness – has to be interpreted as a chapter in his own religious evolution. Later in life he was deeply attracted back to Christianity (and drawn, though not decisively, to Roman Catholicism) and became more alienated from politics, so that George Mackay Brown, remembering him as warden of Newbattle Abbey outside Edinburgh in the 1950s, could remark that: 'I think he never entirely abandoned his youthful socialism, but party politics didn't stir him. He was a Christian but to my knowledge he never entered a church.'[16] There is a sense in which Muir's own political creeds had been so Utopian and his prognosis of the human condition so gloomy in socio-economic terms that logic and emotion were likely to force him back to religion as a private solution. But it was never, in *Scottish Journey* or elsewhere, put forward as a public panacea.

As he goes north into the Highlands he finds a world that is beautiful but emptied by old clearances and broken in its spirit and tradition by its sale to outsiders. Orkney alone, the ultimate destination of his journey, provides a way of life that is prosperous and desirable, but it is impossible for it to be a model to the remainder of Scotland.

His journey north also gives him an excuse to attack (without naming their author) the myths that C.M. Grieve was beginning to propound about a common Celtic heritage to Scottish life in Highland and Lowland alike that was supposed to have given the country a real unity and an essential identity which could be realised and recovered through the discipline of 'Bardic Colleges'.[17] It was a kind of 'back to the Picts' movement which Muir's Orcadian good sense found inherently absurd: 'but even if one were to admit it, and allow that the people were Celtic, they have abundantly shown through many centuries a striking incapacity . . .' Muir did not openly quarrel with Grieve until the following year, when their flyting over the usefulness of Lallans left the Scottish Renaissance with an open wound, but Grieve must have found this first attack treasonable and provoking enough.

So where did Muir's personal quest for the Scottish identity leave him? Not with one clear picture, but with many impressions. There was no distinctive Scotland in Edinburgh, none worth having in small-town life, none that could breathe humanity in the oppression of Glasgow, none that rang true in the kailyard or in the myth-making of Christopher Grieve. There was instead a deeply disunited people, depressed rather than oppressed, quick to resent any insult to Scotland but lethargically incapable of taking any actions to stop its decline. Yet there were still inhabitants of this smashed and emptied country (emptied of population, spirit and innate character) who called themselves Scots and meant by it to distinguish themselves from other peoples. The intentions of the National Party to create self-government were not capable of being opposed by 'serious argument', but unless the system was utterly changed self-government by itself would do little good: 'A

hundred years of socialism would do more to restore
Scotland to health and weld it into a real nation than
a thousand years – if that were conceivable – of
Nationalist government such as that to which the
National Party of Scotland looks forward.'[18] No
Scottish identity worth having will emerge or re-
emerge, in other words, until the crushing weight of
present capitalism is removed, for the root of
Scotland's many ills was not national but economic:
and it is the history of modern economic systems, not
of ancient race (as Grieve with his theory of the
Celtic underfelt was coming perilously close to
saying) that mainly fashions national characteristics.

* * *

Muir's message in 1935, then, was in no way simple
or agreeable, and certainly not flattering to the Scots.

What does it seem like in 1979? Things are in
many respects immeasurably changed since the
1930s, at least in the material sense. Real incomes
per head are not far off double what they were
then. The unemployment rate, though we think it
high now, is only around 8 per cent compared to
the 26 per cent of 1933. Infant mortality, always a
marker of poverty, dropped from 78 deaths per
thousand children under one year old in 1934, to
19 deaths forty years later. The stinking, vermin-
ridden privately owned slums of Glasgow and the
other major cities have been mainly destroyed,

though the council-built tower blocks that replaced them have provided enough bleak problems of a different kind. The working classes shop for their consumer goods along Princes Street without Muir's foretold revolution, and popular car-ownership has banished the pedestrian promenaders (except from the public gardens on summer evenings) as thoroughly as universal access to TV has continued the regional levelling of the cinema and the radio and accentuated the demand for consumer spending.

Much of the change, of course, comes because international capitalism proved itself to be much more resilient than most observers thought possible in 1934, and has gone on producing wealth for distribution among the masses. Part of the change also arises from the spread of interventionist ideas that put the thrust of government action behind welfare and regional policies designed to redress the economic bias against poorer areas. It would be absurd to call these socialist in any sense that Muir would have understood, yet they emerged as a result of a working compromise between those political forces seeking change and those seeking stability.

Equally, it could be argued that in cultural aspects Scotland has not been emptied to the degree Muir assumed that it would be. The creation and success of the Edinburgh Festival must go some way to fulfilling his expressed wish that the capital would one day become a centre for the arts; the creation of

Scottish Opera (with its splendid headquarters at Glasgow), of the Scottish National Orchestra and of Scottish Ballet, the vigour of folk song, and of jazz in Glasgow, the Third Eye Centre there and the Traverse Theatre in Edinburgh are all signs of life in the performing arts absent in the 1930s. Perhaps, at an intellectual level, Muir could not now have stated that 'all Scottish history is inadequate and confusing: it has still to be written'. Beginning with the scholarly labours of Henry Hamilton at Aberdeen in the 1930s, who wrote the first analytical accounts of Scottish economic history, and continuing down to the present day with the work of a score of clamant scholars, the study of the Scottish past has been pursued with a comprehensive seriousness never achieved before. Perhaps only imaginative literature has faltered: for all the patronage of the Scottish Arts Council, few would dare to say that the works of the universal importance of Lewis Grassic Gibbon, of C.M. Grieve, of Edwin Muir himself, or of the early Sorley Maclean have been written in the last twenty years (except perhaps by the curious private head of Edwin Morgan).

On the other hand, at many points Muir's criticisms and observations are still peculiarly correct, and of increasing relevance if the economic climate chills further as the oil runs out. Scotland is still materially much worse off than England in certain important respects, especially in relation to urban deprivation. Despite its progress in the last four decades it has become one of the poorest countries in Europe. The question which exercises the planners in relation to Glasgow (after several failed attempts) is still, in Muir's words, 'How is this collapsing city to be put on its feet again?' The Scottish identity is still as Muir described it, that of a lethargic and divided people, quick to resent a trifling insult but incapable of action to remedy their plight. What other conclusion is possible, when, given the chance to obtain a legislative assembly for the first time since 1707, 32 per cent of the electorate said 'yes', 30 per cent said 'no', and 38 per cent did not trouble to vote at all? It is still a country of Nationalists with no clear or noble social purposes, of a Labour Party with no vision except the retention of power, of Conservatives who know exactly how to play on the people's fear of change, and of drinkers who wrap themselves 'in the safe cloak of alcohol'.

Muir held up a mirror to the face of Scotland forty-five years ago. It is frightening to see so many recognisable features lingering in its glass.

T.C. Smout,
1979

NOTES

1 *Scottish Journey*, p.101
2 For the particulars of Muir's life, see the autobiographies mentioned above, Willa Muir, *Belonging*, and Peter Butter, *Edwin Muir, Man and Poet* (Edinburgh, 1966)
3 Cited in Butter, *op cit*, p.112
4 *The Story and the Fable*, p.263
5 *Belonging*, p.178
6 *Scottish Journey*, p.107
7 *The Story and the Fable*, pp.163–64
8 *Scottish Journey*, p.2
9 *Ibid*, p.149
10 For this see H.J. Hanham, *Scottish Nationalism* (London, 1969), especially Chapter 7
11 *Belonging*, pp.152–53. Butter, *op cit*, pp.124–25
12 H. Belshaw, *The Douglas Fallacy* (Auckland, 1933)
13 C.H. Douglas, *The Douglas Scheme for Scotland* (n.d., n.p.)
14 In a poem called 'Scotland 1941', *The Narrow Place* (London, 1943), p.15
15 Hanham, *op cit*, p.149
16 George Mackay Brown, *Edwin Muir: A Brief Memoir* (West Linton, 1975), p.10
17 See Hanham, *op cit*, p.144
18 *Scottish Journey*, pp.233–34

PREFACE TO THE 1996 EDITION

Many changes have taken place in Scotland since the Preface to the 1979 edition of this book was written. Without a doubt, the nation's cultural life is flourishing. In Alasdair Gray, Janice Galloway and James Kelman one could argue that we are at last seeing writers of the stature of Grieve, Muir and Lewis Grassic Gibbon. The 1980s and 1990s have also given the world of painting new masters in John Bellany, Ken Currie and Peter Howson, whose images of East Coast fishermen, of Scottish stoics, Glasgow dockers and dossers have won universal appeal. Galvanised by Glasgow's year as European City of Culture, there has been a proliferation of festivals and venues – Mayfest, the Royal Concert Hall and the new Gallery of Scottish Art – which has been matched by the capital's new Traverse, the Festival Theatre and planned new Museum of Scotland.

At the same time, however, sixteen years of Conservative rule have seen the gap between the rich and poor grow ever wider, with little hope of redressing the balance. What would Edwin Muir have made of a nation ruled by a party which can only obtain third place in the opinion polls, struggling to keep up with Labour and the Nationalists?

Unemployment figures show few signs of improvement; the Scottish diet, reviled as the most unhealthy in the developed world, is symptomatic of the nation's poverty; homelessness and drug abuse are growing at frightening rates. Unquestionably, there are still strong similarities with the dark, recession-hit Scotland Muir explores in this book.

T.C. Smout
1996

SCOTTISH JOURNEY

THE first thought of writing this book came to me two years ago, one evening after I had driven through the mining district of Lanarkshire. The journey took me through Hamilton, Airdrie and Motherwell. It was a warm, overcast summer day; groups of idle, sullen-looking young men stood at the street corners; smaller groups were wandering among the blue-black ranges of pit-dumps which in that region are the substitute for nature; the houses looked empty and unemployed like their tenants; and the road along which the car stumbled was pitted and rent, as if it had recently been under shell-fire. Everything had the look of a Sunday which had lasted for many years, during which the bells had forgotten to ring and the Salvation Army, with its accordions and concertinas, had gone into seclusion, so that one did not even trouble to put on one's best clothes: a disused, slovenly, everlasting Sunday. The open shops had an unconvincing and yet illicit look, and the few black-dusted miners whom I saw trudging home seemed hardly to believe in their own existence. The scene actually evoked a sense of peace: the groups quietly talking at the street corners or walking among the pit-dumps, the shafts rising smokeless, and the neglected roads.

This was the most impressive scene that I saw in

Scotland, and it is, in the industrial regions, a typical one. A century ago there was a great clearance from the Highlands which still rouses the anger of the people living there. At present, on a far bigger scale, a silent clearance is going on in industrial Scotland, a clearance not of human beings, but of what they depend upon for life. Everything which could give meaning to their existence in these grotesque industrial towns of Lanarkshire is slipping from them; the surroundings of industrialism remain, but industry itself is vanishing like a dream. Airdrie and Motherwell are the most improbable places imaginable in which to be left with nothing to do; for only rough work could reconcile anyone to living in them. Yet a large population lives there in idleness; for there is nowhere else to go, and little prospect that Monday will dawn for a long time.

This is the heart of Scotland, but Scotland is, like all countries, a confusing conglomeration, containing such strange anachronisms as Edinburgh, a great expanse of cultivated and a greater of fallow land, and a number of different races. In the course of my journeyings I came in contact with these various Scotlands, passing from one into another without rhyme or reason, as it seemed to me; but what Scotland is I am still unable to say. It is Edinburgh, certainly, and Airdrie, and Glasgow, and Kirriemuir, and the Kailyard, and the rich agricultural areas of the South, and the depopulated glens of Sutherland, and the prosperous islanded county of Orkney. It has a human

north and south, east and west, as well as a geographical; but though they have been clamped within
a small space for a long time, one feels they have
never met. Then there is the rivalry between Edinburgh and Glasgow, ridiculous in essence, jocular in
expression and acrid in spirit; there are the various
classes, of which I found the working—or rather the
workless—class by far the most honestly admirable;
there are the Socialists, the intellectuals—mostly anti-
Calvinistic, but sentimental compared with their fore-
runners—the Catholics, the Orangemen, the Fascists,
the Nationalists, the hikers, and the churchgoers. Most
of these might be found in any other country, though
the proportions would be different; the intellectuals,
the hikers and the Fascists would be more numerous,
the Socialists and the churchgoers fewer. Finally, cut-
ting across these classifications, come the Highlanders
and the Lowlanders. No two sets of people could be
more temperamentally incompatible. I shall have to
say something about these various divisions in Scottish
life in the course of this book, and perhaps when I
have done that some picture of Scotland will emerge.
But I should like to put here my main impression, and
it is that Scotland is gradually being emptied of its
population, its spirit, its wealth, industry, art, intellect, and innate character. This is a sad conclusion;
but it has some support on historical grounds. If a
country exports its most enterprising spirits and best
minds year after year, for fifty or a hundred or two
hundred years, some result will inevitably follow.

England gives some scope for its best; Scotland gives none; and by now its large towns are composed of astute capitalists and angry proletarians, with nothing that matters much in between. Edinburgh is a partial exception to this; but Edinburgh is a handsome, empty capital of the past. And as no civilisation that is composed merely of exploiters and exploited can endure for long, Glasgow, Dundee, Aberdeen, and Greenock are now following Edinburgh. They are monuments of Scotland's industrial past, historical landmarks in a country which is becoming lost to history.

I should like here to thank the countless friends who have helped me in the making of my journey and the writing of this book, and particularly the donor of the little car without which I should have been helpless. I should warn the reader, too, that this is not a survey of Scotland but a bundle of impressions: not *the* Scottish journey, but *a* Scottish Journey. The three poems I have inserted have already appeared in *The Listener, The New English Weekly* and *Time and Tide,* and my acknowledgements and thanks are due to the editors of these periodicals.

CHAPTER 1

EDINBURGH

I

THE first sight of Edinburgh after an absence is invariably exciting. Its bold and stony look recalls ravines and quarried mountains, and as one's eye runs up the long line of jagged roofs from Holyrood to the Castle, one feels that these house-shapes are outcroppings of the rocky ridge on which they are planted, methodical geological formations in which, as an afterthought, people have taken to living, importing into them tables, chairs, beds, sideboards, wireless sets, and all the other furnishings which make an up-to-date habitation tolerable. The smoke rising from innumerable chimneys produces the same half delightful, half nightmare sense of overcrowding that one finds in mountain villages in Southern Europe, where from what look like mere shallow recesses in the rock issue whole families, accompanied by dogs, cats, and herds of goats. Pigs were once penned in the Canongate, and every evening, when they were driven in from the adjacent fields, they must have made that high and narrow canyon echo with their squealing. The Canongate now is only humanly overcrowded; it is a quiet street, but its silence is slightly menacing; it has the disturbing watchfulness of places where there are too many eyes; innumerable dirty windows with innumerable faces behind them. One passes almost as many people in a walk along Princes Street as in a walk down the Canongate, but the impression is very different, for in the Canongate one is conscious of this second crowd behind the walls. Perhaps it is the height of the houses, the great number and smallness of the windows, and the narrowness of the space in which one has to walk that give this sense of watchfulness and sinister familiarity. But there is in it, too, something of the terror of narrow rocky passes in savage and possibly inhabited regions.

The first, obvious impression that Edinburgh produces is of a rocky splendour and pride. It is a city built upon rock and guarded by rock. The old town is perched on the ridge which runs up from Holyrood to the Castle, and on the other side, to the east, rise the two shapes of the Salisbury Crag and Arthur's Seat. Princes Street with its spacious gardens and its single line of buildings has this magnificent panorama as its missing side.

Behind Princes Street, on the gradual slope running down to the Water of Leith, lies the New Town. This is the town of Hume. Everything in it breathes spaciousness, order and good sense; the houses present a dignified front to the world; they suggest comfortable privacy and are big enough for large parties, and seem admirably planned to withstand the distractions and allow the amenities of a rational city life. The New Town was due to the foresight and enterprise of an Edinburgh provost more than a hundred years ago and to the taste of the architects he employed, and it is probably one of the finest pieces of town-planning extant. It shows that a little over a hundred years ago Edinburgh possessed a boldness of foresight and a standard of achievement which at that time were remarkable.

Taken together the Old Town and the New produce an effect of spacious design. The design of the Old Town is a result of the rocky formation which is its base, the design of the New purely architectural. The Old Town is by now mostly slums, and parts of the New are falling into the same state. Beyond this nucleus of the city lie Victorian, Edwardian and Neo-Georgian suburbs, most of them, and the last more particularly, shapeless and graceless. In these the great majority of the population live.

It was in Edinburgh that I started on my discovery of Scotland. I had often been in it for short visits during the years that I lived as a young man in Glasgow. At that time I had never been outside Scotland, and, except for a rather sentimental reverence for its historical buildings, and the memories adhering to them, I found little in the capital to strike me. I think one has to come from a different country, a country as different as England, to appreciate it properly.

One's final impression of a town is coloured by all the emotions one has ever felt in it and probably by many which one has completely forgotten. My visit to Edinburgh last summer was the last of several dozens that I had paid to it at one time or another. The later of these visits did not so much add to my knowledge of the town as reawaken a whole series of memories and pictures, and I find now that I cannot give any idea of Edinburgh without going back to the first morning I spent in it when I was fourteen.

This first impression, though fragmentary and dream-like, has the advantage of being far more vivid than any of my later ones, perhaps because I had not yet accumulated literary and historical reminiscences to obscure what I actually saw. The whole town was also an unforetellable surprise to me, for I arrived in it straight from the Orkney Islands, where I had never seen a train, a tram-car, a factory, a tenement, a theatre, a slum, or any of the other normal features of a modern city. I have two memories of that first sight of Edinburgh. The first is of a walk with one of my brothers through a very long, neat, glittering-windowed and stony terrace, with steps running up to the doors, and gates opening on the pavement. Later came a green hill with a number of monuments scattered over it, and after that we were suddenly in a very chill and formal and huge building. All that I can remember of it is a statue of a naked woman inside the door. Two dirty boys of about my own age were standing sniggering in front of it and glancing every now and then at a particular point on it. I looked for a long time, and saw at last that this was a great black thumb-mark on

8

one of the breasts of the statue. The place was dark, for the morning was a dull one; and all the rest of that gallery, which I must have walked through, is plunged in complete oblivion now.

That first half-blind glimpse of Edinburgh happened by chance to catch one thing about it which anyone accustomed to cities would probably not have seen: that it is a city of extraordinary and sordid contrasts. The tourist's eye is a very specialised mechanism, and it is quite capable of such apparently impossible feats as taking in the ancient monuments and houses of Edinburgh without noticing that they are filthy and insanitary. Yet the historical part of Edinburgh, the part most frequented by visitors, is a slum intersected by ancient houses that have been segregated and turned into museums and training-colleges. Most of the Canongate is a mouldering and obnoxious ruin. The stone of the houses looks diseased, as if it were decaying not with old age, but with some sort of dirty scurvy produced by poverty, filth and long-continued sorrow. The street itself, on fine days, is thronged with groups of young men. But the crowds are stationary, for every inducement that might make them leave the corner where they stand has long since ceased to exist. In Princes Street people walk, for they have money, and along with it hope and a host of effectual desires; but in the Canongate they stand, or when they are tired of that sit on the pavement in groups with their feet out on the causeway. Some of them must have stood and sat like this for a decade. Last July, when I saw them, they looked as brown as if they had been all summer at the sea-side, for the weather had been fine for several weeks.

In spite of its proud display, then, Edinburgh cannot hide away its unemployed or its poor. Yet as it is a city which must keep up appearances, there are certain rules which it does not like to see broken. It accepts the unemployed groups in the Canongate without visible annoyance; but when about a year ago a procession of the unemployed stopped in the town on their way to London, and slept for the night in Princes Street gardens, there was general indignation, in the tea-rooms, the tram-cars and the columns of the local newspapers; for people's sense of propriety was outraged.

A town is like a very big and inefficiently yet strictly run house. The work in this house is done in the most haphazard way; good servants are ill-treated and badly paid, and dishonest servants praised and coddled; and the refuse which every big house continuously produces is not decently disposed of and hidden away as it is in most big houses, but barefacedly dumped some distance away in full view of the public yet where the master is not likely to stumble into it. All this is done with the most cynical inefficiency; but on the other hand the servants have to submit to the strictest regulation, both in their working hours and their leisure. They have their quarters, for instance, to which they must keep. They must on no account sprawl about in the drawing-room, even in their spare time. If their

windows should happen to look out on the general
refuse-heap, it is merely a geographical accident. Their
windows look one way, their master's the other. By this
parable I merely wish to point a fact which has often
astonished me: that is, the complete success with which,
in a large town, everything is kept in its place. There
are streets in Edinburgh which correspond exactly to
the drawing-room and the servants' hall. The people
one meets in the first are quite different from the
people one meets in the second. The crowds that walk
along Princes Street, for instance, are a different race,
different in their manners, their ideas, their feelings,
their language, from the one in the Canongate. The
distance between the two streets is trifling; the difference between the crowds enormous. And it is a constant and permanent difference. You never by chance
find the Princes Street crowd in the Canongate, or the
Canongate crowd in Princes Street; and without a
revolution such a universal American Post is inconceivable. The entire existence of Edinburgh as a
respectable bourgeois city depends on that fact.
Nothing more than a convention is involved, but the
conventions on which a society rests easily become
sacred; and so a wholesale invasion of Princes Street
by the poor would be felt not only as an offence against
good taste, but as a blasphemy. That is why the temporary presence of the unemployed there was so deeply
resented and feared.

But one does not need to go so far as the Canongate to see this curious principle in full operation.

Within a stone's throw of one end of Princes Street
begins a promenade quite different in character. This
is Leith Street and its continuation Leith Walk, a long
spacious boulevard containing some fine old houses,
which have with time sunk to the status of working-
class tenements. Here, instead of the cosy tea-rooms
and luxurious hotel lounges of Princes Street, one suddenly finds oneself among ice-cream and fish-and-chip
bars and pubs. At one point the two different streams
of promenaders are brought within a few yards of each
other; yet they scarcely ever mingle, so strong is the
sense of social distinction bred by city life. They turn
back when they reach this invisible barrier, apparently
without thought or desire, as if they were stalking in a
dream; and if, through necessity or whim, an occasional
pedestrian should trespass for a little on enemy ground,
he is soon frightened and scurries back as fast as he can.
The prostitutes are the sole class who rise superior to
this inhibition. They live, as members of the proletariat, in the poorer districts, but their main beat is
Princes Street, and it has in their eyes the prestige and
familiarity of a business address. But their occupation
seems to be the sole remaining one in modern society
which acts as a general dissolvent of all social distinctions; and that in reality is because they are tacitly out-
lawed by all society, in which the principle of class
distinction is constantly operative. The ordinary
crowds, not possessing this classless power, turn back
at a certain point. The upper and lower middle classes,
the men about town, clerks, commercial travellers,

students, patrol Princes Street, because, without being conscious of it, they look upon that walk as a preserve where they can be at their complete ease, and where nobody will ever intrude upon them. And this calculation is justified. Their seclusion is as perfect as if they were behind locked doors.

I can give an instance of how this law works. One Saturday evening last July I was taking a walk down Princes Street with my wife and a visitor from Serbia. The pubs had just closed, for it was after ten, and Princes Street was crowded but orderly. As soon as we turned into Leith Street we came upon a group of drunk men arguing loudly on the pavement. A little later we encountered two handsome young women, fashionably dressed, and obviously prostitutes, who were having a hand-to-hand fight and screaming abuse at each other. A ring had formed round them, and presently one of them was knocked flat on her back, at which a man intervened and stopped the fight. Thereupon the two young women dusted their clothes, powdered their faces, and made off quietly towards Princes Street, which was within a stone's throw; their altered demeanour showing that they were entering their business quarter, where they could not afford to indulge such a trivial luxury as a private quarrel; they might almost have been going to an important conference or to church. The Serbian said it was the first fight between women that he had ever seen, and asked whether this was a national custom. I told him that I did not think so.

Scottish streets are given an atmosphere of their own simply by the number of drunk people that one encounters in them. Whether the Scottish people drink more than other peoples it would be impossible to say; but they give the impression of doing so, because of the abundant signs of public drunkenness that one finds in such towns as Edinburgh and Glasgow and even in small country towns on a Saturday night. During a fortnight's stay in Edinburgh I did not get through a single evening without seeing at least one example of outrageous or helpless drunkenness, and I had spent two years in London without coming across more than four or five. I think the explanation is that Scottish people drink spasmodically and intensely, for the sake of a momentary but complete release, whereas the English like to bathe and paddle about bucolically in a mild puddle of beer. One might put down this difference to a difference of national temperament or of national religion or to a hundred other things; there is no doubt, in any case, that the drinking habits of the Scots, like their dances, are far wilder than those of the English. The question is not a very important or interesting one. Much more interesting is the difference which class distinction produces in drunkenness in a Scottish town. There are as many drunk men and women in Princes Street on a Saturday night as in Leith Walk. But there are far fewer signs of them, and this is mainly due to social causes. Even when a man is in other ways incapable, he tries to conform to his particular code of manners, and so drunken-

ness in Princes Street is quiet and genteel: shown
in a trifling unsteadiness of gait or a surprising
affability of aspect by which the middle-class Edinburgh man manages to suggest that he is somehow up-
holding something or other which distinguishes him
from the working classes. He is helped in this purpose
by certain benevolent external circumstances, however, such as that the whisky sold in Princes Street is
better than the whisky one buys in Leith Walk, and
that it is always easy to get a taxi in Princes Street
after ten o'clock. By means of these discreet
ambulances the unconscious and semi-conscious are
inconspicuously removed. In Leith Walk they lie
about the pavement until their friends or the police
laboriously lead them away. Thus appearances are
kept up, appearances upon which a whole host of the
most important things depend.

There is far more street life in the large Scottish
cities than there is, for instance, in London. Why this
should be so, I do not know; perhaps it is a relic of
French influence, which was once powerful in Scotland; but a more probable explanation is that, in a
country of few amusements, and these mostly frowned
on, walking out to see the world acquired the rank of
a rare pleasure. Indoor enjoyment is now cheap and
accessible in Edinburgh; there are countless cinemas
and tea-rooms and pubs, as well as dance-halls; but the
habit of walking the streets and looking at the world
is still an essential part of Scottish town life. This out-
door habit makes life in Scotland less enclosed, less an

exclusively private affair than it is in England. The people in the streets at least look at one another. Though their contacts may be rare and fleeting, they are aware of themselves as a moving spectacle; and no eccentricity in a passer-by, for example, escapes them. This frank and eager sightseeing generates a sort of exhilaration, which is not very intense, but is rather like the subdued expectation in a theatre before the curtain goes up, when the audience is conscious of itself as an unexpectedly intimate entity.

This expectation can be felt quite distinctly in the intentness of the street crowds in Scottish cities, and it is quite natural, for the mere act of waiting makes one more conscious of the people about one. The most pre-occupied business man will gaze inquisitively at every-body who passes him on a country platform where he has been forced to waste half an hour, though he would not spend a glance on the same people if he were on his way to his office. Princes Street in the evening is like a country platform where the train is late; there is the same intense and permitted scrutiny of one's fellow-passengers, the same growing expectation, and behind these the same sense, too, or rather a greater one, of weariness and prolonged disappointment. For the train never arrives at this platform, and so waiting becomes a thing with an existence of its own, which can no longer call up any definite image such as the arrival of a train, and is forced to find alleviation finally in distractions, in temporary liaisons with one's stranded companions. Perhaps in the background there persists a faith that a train will arrive some day, an unimaginable train such as the world has never seen before. But prolonged waiting breeds frustration and finally resignation; and a man gets used to his platform and finds it is after all a tolerable place, where he can take his pleasure as well as in any other. Until at last he grows weary of it, retires definitely, into matrimony perhaps, and leaves the field to passengers younger, more sanguine and more expectant than himself.

One of the advantages of this platform life is that it increases people's powers of observation, and of resistance to observation. In Princes Street you are seen, whoever you may be, and this knowledge, partly alarming and partly exhilarating like a plunge into cold water, forces the pedestrian to assemble his powers and be as intent as his neighbours. The concentrated force of observation sent out by the people he passes is sometimes so strong that he has the feeling of breaking, as he passes, through a series of invisible obstacles, of snapping a succession of threads laden with some retarding current. In London he can walk the most crowded streets for hours without feeling that he is either visible or existent: a disconcerting, almost frightening experience for a Scotsman until he gets used to it. But the crowd in a London street is mainly composed of people who are going somewhere, while the crowd in Princes Street is simply there; and even if you are going somewhere you cannot ignore it; it acquisitively stretches out and claims you. For it is there not only to observe, but also to be observed, and if you omit one of these duties you strike at its *amour-propre*, and perhaps at its existence. If a continuous relay of absent-minded philosophers could be let loose in Princes Street, the very foundations of its life would be shaken, and it would either rise and massacre these innocent revolutionaries or else die of disappointment.

This apparently unmotivated intentness of Scottish street crowds is filled with unsatisfied desire. It is as if the eye were trying to undertake the functions of all the other senses, and the accumulated frustration and hope of a people were thrown into a painfully concentrated look. In such unnatural circumstances the eye acquires an almost prehensile power; it flings out invisible tentacles which draw its victims to it and into it, so that it can devour, digest and excrete them with lightning rapidity. This process resembles a sort of reciprocal and incorporeal massacre, in which eater and eaten remain unchanged. It is finally a little exhausting, for such a diet does not allay hunger; after the thousandth meal the eye remains as starved as after the first: it may in the course of time assume a brazen, defiant, even a pleading expression, but it is always unsatiated.

This yearning again is drenched in unsatisfied sex. Nowhere that I have been is one so bathed and steeped and rolled about in floating sexual desire as in certain streets of Glasgow and Edinburgh. This desire fills the main thoroughfare and overflows into all the adjacent pockets and backwaters: the tea-rooms, restaurants and cinema lounges. The only refuges from it are the pubs, which convention forbids women to enter, but which, nevertheless, are always well attended. There, like sailors after a difficult and nerve-whipping voyage, the men put into harbour and wrap themselves in the safe cloak of alcohol, which Luther thought such a secure defence against the flesh. But those whom Princes Street leaves still unsatisfied resort to the tea-rooms and lounges, where they languidly steep themselves until they are quite saturated. Among the tea-rooms in Princes Street there are places more strange than a dream. Passing through a corridor one enters an enormous room filled with dull and glassy light, and as silent as if it were miles under-sea. Nereids float in the submarine glimmer, bearing trays in their hands; and over glassy tables the drowned sway like seaweeds, the sluggish motion of the tide turning their heads now this way, now that, with an effect of hypnotic ogling. When one gets used to the light one sees that these amphibious sea-plant-like forms are respectable members of the Edinburgh bourgeoisie, that their clothes are quite dry, and that the sea change they have suffered is temporary, having been paid for. They are well-dressed people, and they are drinking tea and eating scones.

You fly from these dim recesses if you fear darkness and silence. At your next attempt you may be plunged into equatorial glare and din. You seem to be on a tropical island, or a pleasure-boat contentedly

stranded on some Sargasso Sea. The sounds that come
from the band make you plump for the latter supposi-
tion, and you see that the players, to enhance the holiday illusion, are wearing light flannels with red sashes
round their waists. But, looking at the walls, you
change your mind again: there the jungle waves, lions
and tigers leap out every moment, spears hurtle
through the air, and in peaceful clearings lovely girls,
of a light biscuit brown, gaze out in immobile desire.
The light blinds, the music deafens, and walls fling
themselves at you: you are punched, pummelled and
rolled over and over by a torrent of harsh noise and
colour. Amid all this turmoil waitresses in neat
Kailyard dresses bustle about, bearing ham and eggs,
Welsh rabbits, scones, cakes, fruit salad, lemonade,
stone ginger-beer, and ice-cream. For the crowning
touch to these places is that they are teetotal. They
excite or depress the senses to the limit of endurance,
and pour non-alcoholic drinks on the resulting commo-
tion. The pubs are, in comparison, civilised and
humane institutions.

The tastelessness and vulgarity of the Edinburgh
tea-rooms strike one with all the greater force because
of the beauty of the town itself. Edinburgh has a style,
and that style was at one time, indeed as recently as a
century ago, the reflection of a whole style of life.
While the city itself remains, this style of life has now
been broken down, or rather submerged, by successive
waves of change which were first let loose during the
Industrial Revolution, an event that has on a large scale

swept from the great towns of Europe the innate character which they once possessed. The waves have almost completely submerged London; but Edinburgh, being a high, angular place, is more difficult to drown. So it presents outwardly the face it had a hundred years ago, while within it is worm-eaten with all the ingenuity in tastelessness which modern resources can supply.

A town was once as natural an expression of a people's character as its landscape and its fields; it sprang up in response to a local and particular need; its houses, churches, and streets were suited to the habits and nature of the people who lived in it. Industrialism, which is a mechanical cosmopolitan power —and the same in Prague as in Glasgow—has changed this. It makes people live in houses which do not suit them, work in places which two hundred years ago would have been considered as mad as a nightmare, and destroys their sense even of ordinary suitability; and it does all this because its motive force is a mechanical and not a human one. Anyone, for example, should be able to see that the approach to Holyrood should not be through a barrage of smoke from breweries; but Industrialism has so corrupted us that we take that now as a matter of course. Edinburgh is not predominantly an industrial town, and so one does not find in it the universal massacre of style that one finds, for instance, in Glasgow. But that massacre is carried on very efficiently in the genteel tea-rooms and hotel lounges. These places have no geographical

connection with Edinburgh; they might be almost anywhere in the No Man's Land of bad taste, if it were
not for the fact that they remind one of other capitals
of twenty years ago, that they are dated.

As the tea-room is an institution of Edinburgh, a
convention through which the middle and upper
middle classes express themselves, it deserves further
notice. The effect that these places are designed to produce is one of luxury, and the more select of them
strive for an impression of adroitly muffled silence,
silence being in an industrial civilisation, which is the
noisiest known form of civilisation, the supreme
evidence of luxury because the most difficult thing to
achieve. Into this silence the discreet sounds of the
radio may be safely decanted, for that is a controlled
and deliberate noise, which requires this silky silence
as its foundation and is itself only an added proof of
luxury. The luxury is intended to build up a decep-
tion, to lead the hypnotically blissful tea-drinker to
the mistaken conclusion that here is something as good
as the richest and the most leisured can enjoy. So while
the actual material of the banquet may be simple, a
harsh brew of Indian tea gulped with scones and cakes,
the surroundings must show in every detail that they
are better than they have any need to be. This, as far
as I have been able to make out, is the calculation on
which all the more stylish tea-rooms in Edinburgh are
run; a perfectly justified calculation, the desire for
luxury being almost universal and taste a very rare
possession. The people who frequent these places seem

to be mainly middle-class, that is people with ideas above their station; there is a clear majority of women, and among them a surprising number of old ladies. The men, I fancy, belong chiefly to the class of clerical workers, who do not know very clearly where they stand in the economic hierarchy, who yearn, almost legitimately, for the luxury of the wealthy, but by some unexplained mistake have to spend their lives in poor lodgings. The working class, the trade union and class-conscious proletariat, do not often enter such places.

As I write this, it strikes me that I am not describing a Scottish scene at all. And that is true, simply because terms like Scottish and English are becoming less and less descriptive of any form of life. So although Edinburgh is Scottish in itself, one cannot feel that the people who live in it are Scottish in any radical sense, or have any essential connection with it. They do not even go with it; they look like visitors who have stayed there for a long time. One imagines that not very long ago the real population must have been driven out, and that the people one sees walking about came to stay in the town simply because the houses happened to be empty. In other words, one cannot look at Edinburgh without being conscious of a visible crack in historical continuity. The actual town, the houses, streets, churches, rocks, gardens, are there still; but these exist wholly in the past. That past is a national past; the present, which is made up of the thoughts and feelings and prejudices of the inhabitants, their way of life in general, is as cosmopolitan as the cinema. This is not universally true; but it applies to the populace, rich and poor, the great multitude who have been Anglicised and Americanised, whether by the film, the Press, the radio, the lending library, or the public schools. There are people who still maintain the old Edinburgh tradition, which, if a little cold and stony like the town itself, has seriousness and dignity. But these are in a small minority, like every section in the Scottish towns which still thinks in Scottish terms. The various agencies I have mentioned have brought about a radical and silent revolution; and the present inhabitants of Edinburgh are as different from the inhabitants of fifty years ago as the Americans now are from the English. They are better in some ways, no doubt, less rigid and hard, and less bigoted; but they do not think in what one might call an Edinburgh way, as their forefathers did. The only remnant of Scottish custom that remains among them is their street life, and how long it will continue to resist the radio, which has done so much to consolidate the home by bringing all the world into it, is hard to say.

The effect of all such innovations as the movies and the wireless is to make the place people stay in of less and less importance. Immediate environment has no longer, therefore, the shaping effect that it used to have; the inhabitants of all our towns, great and small, Scottish and English, are being subjected more and more exclusively to action from a distance, and, which is more important, to the same action from the same distance. This is a great revolution, and in part, no doubt, a beneficial one. But the freedom which the radio offers has the illusoriness of spiritualistic messages; it breaks a path into a new dimension of space, but the voice that reaches us from that world is the voice of everyman, everyman carefully groomed, on his best behaviour, at his most civil, invisible and invulnerable; the perfect, discreetly distilled extract of everyman. Such a phenomenon has never been known in history before our day, and what effect the utterances of this extraordinary ghost will eventually have upon us is past imagination. It will probably be an improving effect; but one can safely say that it is not likely to encourage variety and originality of character, as the older state of things did, before the appearance of the popular newspaper. For variety and originality of character are produced by an immediate and specific environment; and that, in modern life, counts for less and less; it is being disintegrated on every side, and seems to be, indeed, a life-form of the past. It would be idle to regret this process, since it is inevitable.

This great change is nevertheless disquieting to many people; and it was mainly to combat it, I think, that the Scottish National Party came into existence. Though Scotland has not been a nation for some time, it has possessed a distinctly marked style of life; and that is now falling to pieces, for there is no visible and effective power to hold it together. There is such a visible and effective power to conserve the life of England; and though in English life, too, a similar change of national characteristics is going on, though the old

England is disappearing, there is no danger that England should cease to be itself. But all that Scotland possesses is its style of life; once it loses that it loses everything, and is nothing more than a name on a map. The question arises whether that style of life is worth conserving, and therefore whether something should be done to conserve it. That is a question which can be decided ultimately only by the Scots people themselves, though for its effectual solution the understanding and help of England are needed. It would be foolish to claim that the Scottish style of life is inherently better than the English; in most ways it is less admirable; but it is a style with laws of its own, which it must obey if it is to achieve anything of genuine worth.

Everybody knows that the Scotsman who tries to be English takes on the worst English qualities and exaggerates them to caricature. And the vowel-clipping, flag-wagging, Empire-trumpeting Scotsman is, I think, not a fantastic example of what the Scottish race in general might become if it were submitted unconditionally to English influence. For the Scottish character has a thoroughness, or in other words an inability to know where to stop, which is rarely found in Englishmen, who make a virtue of compromise. When Scotsmen become English they do it with this thoroughness; they work out the English character, which has the vaguest connection with logic, to its logical conclusion, to something, in other words, which only formally resembles it, and is in spirit completely

different. They do this on insufficient knowledge and
with the aggressive confidence which is one of the
curses of the Scottish character, and produce with
elation a botched copy of a warped original. This
process is called Anglicisation, and it is going on
rapidly among the upper classes in Scotland. It is
clearly harmful to both countries, and it is bound to
become more harmful as it continues.

The great mass of Scotsmen and women have not
reached this stage. They are not conscious of English
influence, and they have certainly no wish to become
English. The possession of an accent approximately
English is certainly regarded by them as a mark of social
and intellectual superiority. But that is mainly because
English is the language of the schools, the universities,
the pulpits, the business world, the Press, and finally
of the Bible itself, which, though it is not read now as
widely as in the past, has had a deep influence on
Scottish ways of thought, even about English, and has,
through centuries of usage, engendered a reverence for
that tongue. The ability to speak English is an accom-
plishment, however, and little more; and though it may
bring with it a slight contempt for colloquial Scots, as
a language suitable only for humble needs, it does not
involve any wish or any intention of becoming English
or denying the Scottish tradition. And besides, English
as it is spoken in Scotland is very different from English, and certainly very full of Scottish character.

What makes the existence of the mass of the people
in Scotland so unsatisfactory, apart from their economic

plight (which is the only urgent question: I shall come to it later), is not the feeling that they are being subjected to English influence, but rather the knowledge that there is no Scottish influence left to direct them. They are not English, and they are ceasing to be Scottish for lack of encouragement. They live in the sort of vacuum which, one imagines, exists in the provincial towns of Austrian Italy, or of German Poland: in places that have lost their old life and have not yet found a new one. A certain meaninglessness and despondency hangs round such places; they are out of things; they do not know the reason for their existence; and people emigrate from them readily, without knowing why. The increasing centralisation of all vital energies in London has turned Scotland more and more into a place of this kind. A hundred years ago it still led a life of its own; it no longer does so, except in remote regions, and an impalpable atmosphere of dejection is spread over it.

It was, then, to make way against this internal ailment that the Scottish Nationalist movement came into existence. To some people the very name of Nationalism is hateful; it is over-weening and dangerous in a great nation, and niggling in a small one; trying either to set up a world empire, or to establish a provincial caucus. No doubt Nationalism is the symptom of a morbid state, since it springs either from inflated pride, as it did in England's Jingo days, or from a sense of oppression, or from a mixture of both, as in present-day Germany. When it springs from pride it is a general danger; but when it is caused by a local injustice it loses its virulence once the injustice is removed. The unfortunate thing for Scotland is that it is not an obviously oppressed nation, as Ireland was, but only a visibly depressed one searching for the source of its depression. Glencoe and Culloden are things of the distant past, useful perhaps for a peroration or the refrain of a song, but with no bearing on the present state of things, since everybody can see the English and the Scots living side by side in peace. In such circumstances Nationalism becomes an argument supported by reason on the one side and met with scepticism on the other. Yet in spite of that Scotland is as urgently in need of independence as Ireland was. More urgently, indeed, for if she does not get it she will lose her national consciousness, as Ireland would never have done.

I do not believe that Scotland will ever become a nation by the adoption of Nationalism; I shall explain my reasons for this belief at a later stage. But the nationalist argument is perfectly reasonable as far as it goes. The remedy which Nationalists prescribe for the ills of Scotland is self-government. There is, to anyone who knows the state of Scotland, no serious argument against it. The National Party of Scotland does not wish to cast loose from England; all that it claims is that in domestic matters Scotland should rule itself. This policy is so moderate that bills embodying it have repeatedly passed a first reading in the House of Commons. The great majority of Scottish Members of

Parliament for many years have been in favour of it. Yet in spite of that nothing has been done; partly no doubt because Scotland is such a distance from Westminster. What stands in the way of Home Rule for Scotland is simply apathy, the apathy of England, but chiefly the apathy of Scotland. Consequently the Scottish Nationalist movement at its present stage is mainly a movement to rouse Scotland from its indifference, an attempt to quicken national life and bring about an internal regeneration. There are faint signs that it is beginning to succeed, but its success is slow, and the great mass of the population are still sunk in indifference. They are quick to resent any insult to Scotland, but do not see the necessity of taking any action to stop their country's decline, for, being already half denationalised, they are almost unconscious of the danger.

This short digression is necessary for any understanding of the present state of Scottish life, particularly in the towns. It is an unsatisfied, yearning, morbidly expectant life. And in Edinburgh, where the past is so strong, and the memory of Scottish history is perpetually reminding you, if you are a Scotsman, that this was once a capital, the half-meaninglessness of Scottish life overwhelms you more strongly than anywhere else. The Scots have always been an unhappy people; their history is a varying record of heroism, treachery, persistent bloodshed, perpetual feuds, and long-winded and sanguine arguments ending in such ludicrous sackends as Bothwell Brig. But they were once discontentedly unhappy, and they are now, at

least the better off of them, almost contentedly so.
And this acceptance of the sordid third or fourth best,
imported from every side, is what oppresses one so
much as one walks down their streets.

II

I had not been long in Edinburgh before I began
to formulate the conclusion that the social life of the
people, and particularly of the upper classes, was the
result of ever so many causes of which they were for
the most part unaware. If one knew enough about the
general life of a Scottish town, and especially about its
economic life, one should be able to elaborate an
interesting and illuminating theory of Scottish
manners. One would certainly have to take the past
history of Scotland into account in doing this, perceiv-
ing the influence of Knox and Melville in the stiffness
and formality of Scottish public functions, and of past
poverty in the extraordinarily rich display of all kinds
of solid foods. One would trace the provinciality of
these functions to Scotland's loss of nationality; their
uneasiness to Scotland's vacillation between the rival
claims of rank, culture and money as the real standard
of social eligibility; and their lack of grace to the fact
that most people in Scotland, rich and poor, live in
fairly close contact with an Industrial System which
sardonically eliminates the graces of life. All these
defects may be found in the social life of Edinburgh,

and for some such set of reasons, it seems to me, as I have tried to indicate; but to demonstrate this would require an enormous body of knowledge as well as the closest reasoning. I shall have to content myself, in the absence of these, with retailing the impressions of an intelligent foreigner who last summer had a good taste of Edinburgh social life. His impressions were more unbiassed and objective than mine could be. On the other hand, they were somewhat amateurish, since he had very little close acquaintance with Scottish life, and could only put his finger on results without understanding causes. I shall try to correct and criticise his conclusions as I go on, and in that way bring them nearer to fact.

This foreigner, a young man, came to Edinburgh to attend an international conference of writers, and he was invited to several receptions given by various public bodies. He was most impressed of all by what seemed to him the close resemblance between the Edinburgh people and the English. He had been to Wales for a few days before coming to Scotland, and there he had felt that he was in a completely different country, while Edinburgh seemed to him a mere outpost of England. I think only a foreigner would have made this mistake, but that he could have done so at all shows how much Edinburgh has been Anglicised. Stendhal, during his visit to Edinburgh about a century ago, was astonished in the opposite way, and while cursing the Scottish Sabbath as the most adequate image of Hell that he had found, was filled with amazement at the difference in character between the Scots and the English. There is no doubt that he would be less amazed to-day.

The second thing that struck my friend was the abundance, the ostentation, but in one important respect the circuitousness of Edinburgh hospitality. On entering the halls to which he was invited his eyes were invariably met by vast piles of food of the best, most nutritive and most appetising kind; but there was no evidence of alcoholic drink in any form. My friend is an abstemious man, but the lack of balance in this banquet nevertheless disconcerted him; and he would have left the country under the grave error, he told me, if a kindly Scotsman had not taken him by the arm, led him down various corridors and round various corners, and ushered him at last into a little room where whisky, beer and several other kinds of drink were freely flowing. This arrangement charmed him, and he was inclined at first to think that it was a surprise deliberately rehearsed for foreign guests. But on going to the other receptions he found the same arrangement repeated with minor alterations, involving the climbing of stairs which he had not seen until they were pointed out, and similar feats. He now decided that the drinks were hidden away in this curious manner that the excitement of discovering them might melt what stiffness the company would otherwise have felt. A quaint and essentially hospitable custom, he decided, but hard on the ladies.

My friend returned with curious persistence to this

custom, on which, I believe, he intends to write one of those amusing semi-philosophical essays which have given him a name in his own country. I would find him murmuring, when he thought I was not listening: "But hard on the ladies." For the feat of discovering the drinks is undertaken only by the more robust of the males, and once they have succeeded it must be confessed that they show no great inclination to divulge their secret, particularly to the female half of the guests. An open secret, after all, is no secret, but, being a tender-hearted man, my friend could not forget the sad plight of the great female majority. I found it impossible, after several attempts, to enlighten him on this point.

Another thing which struck him—and it also supported his theory, which I have just outlined—was what he called the excessive stiffness combined with excessive conviviality of Edinburgh society. He had the impression, he told me, that he had shaken many Bailies' hands in the most solemn way and drunk with many Bailies in the most hilarious way. This stiffness and its total disappearance equally puzzled him, and he was at a loss in which to believe. He was not sure, it might have been a trick of memory, but on looking back he imagined he could recall a sort of incipient wink in the Bailie frozen, which was a future promise of the Bailie thawed. But he did not know how to interpret this masonic sign, and for the moment, he confessed, it added a solemn significance to the formal hand-shaking which quite overwhelmed him. Your

Bailie, he told me, is a good fellow at heart, but there is a division in his nature; he is simultaneously proud and ashamed of the part he is playing; and the result is that he is by turns, or even in the same breath, too dignified and too undignified. Our friend, he went on, beneath his rude exterior (he actually used such phrases, being a great admirer of the English eighteenth-century writers) is consideration itself; yet I must admit that I felt shocked when I saw him kissing the pretty best-seller in the bar. Whether it is that your public life is too private, or your private life too public, I cannot say; it may be that I am morbidly sensitive about such things, being accustomed to the stricter continental standards of public propriety.

I report only a few of the many interesting observations made by my friend. As I look back on them, they present such an inextricable tangle of penetration and misunderstanding that I find it almost impossible to isolate the few strands of truth. My friend's theory of the drinks, for instance, is, I think, largely mistaken and founded on what I must call a comprehensive ignorance of Scottish life. Everybody who knows Scotland knows that Scotsmen delight to infuse something of secrecy, something almost masonic, into their potations. They invariably know of a place, which is always round a corner; and thither, nursing their secret to the last minute, they lead you with a discoverer's circumspection and pride. There, like a company of souls reborn by Freud, they resoundingly let fall their inhibitions, and in their chosen cenacle are new men in the twinkling of an eye. I imagine it is the highly developed critical faculty of the Scots that explains this cult of secrecy in drinking. Many things have gone to develop that general critical temper; the tradition of street life, which is still alive, and the past discipline of Presbyterianism, whose foundation was a universal vigilance: the function of the elders having been to keep a strict watch on the congregation and the minister, of the congregation to dog the steps of the minister and the elders, and of the minister to have his eye on everybody. The records of the Kirk Sessions show how complete and crushing was this surveillance; and though the Kirk Sessions are now happily a past terror, the habit of severe criticism still remains, so that Scotsmen feel they can only be free in secret and chosen haunts. The atmosphere of truancy which clings round this style of drinking, making it a forbidden and yet legitimate pleasure, is, I think, peculiar to Scotland.

This, then, I am certain, explains the curious arrangement of the drinks at the receptions, which so puzzled my continental friend. It was an immovable piece of Scottish history that confronted him there, not a mere refinement of social etiquette. The corners he had to circumnavigate were predestined corners, whose architects were John Knox, Andrew Melville, Thomas Boston, and many an unknown Kirk Session which once struck terror into the hearts of its parish; and he is to be excused if behind these humble obstacles he failed to perceive the formidable shape of history. The character of a people comes out in the most trifling expressions of its life, and my friend showed a true sense of proportion in seizing upon the problem of the drinks, though his theory was inadequate. He had to search for them because drinking is in Scotland a secret mainly confined to the masculine sex. The mystery of the Bailie which teased him was quite a simple one. He was confronted in turn by the public Bailie and the secret Bailie, the Bailie in chains, civic and other, and the Bailie unbound.

There is one form which this intimate freedom of the Scots takes that is completely delightful. My friend was especially enthusiastic about the small parties which always followed the public receptions, and as I, too, was fortunate enough to be invited to one or two of them I can corroborate his praise. The breaking up of huge public functions in Edinburgh is not unlike a dignified and orderly shipwreck; one moment, my friend told me, you feel yourself adrift on the bleak waves; in the next a friendly hand has hauled you to safety and comfort. These little parties timed with such witty precision start thus with every advantage. The guests feel that they have survived a severe strain and escaped an unknown danger; and they are in a mood to relax, while they forget, or better still relate, their past hardships.

I had the good fortune to be at one or two of those parties, or Ceilidhs, as they call them, and I have seldom enjoyed anything more. They have no English equivalent. They are free without the affectation of Bohemianism. If one's sole acquaintance with Scotland were through them, one would be forced to believe that Scotsmen and Scotswomen were the most charming and light-hearted people in the world. Their particular charm consists in perfect effortlessness, combined with perfect restraint. A Ceilidh is a small party with music. But everything was so spontaneous, or appeared to be so, that the songs seemed a mere flowering of the general mood. There was no set programme and no sign of awkward improvisation. I think an English company could not be so free-hearted without feeling foolish or self-conscious; but at certain happy moments, in the first relief after a hardship passed, there are companies in Scotland which can strike this perfect balance between nature and art.

My impressions of Edinburgh, or rather of historical Scotland, my feeling of the contrast between its legendary past and its tawdry present, crystallised several months after my visit in a poem, which I set here as an end-piece.

Now the frost lays its smooth claws on the sill,
The sun looks from the hill
Helmed in his winter casket
And sweeps his arctic sword across the sky.
The water at the mill
Sounds more hoarse and dull.
The miller's daughter walking by

With frozen fingers soldered to her basket
Seems to be knocking
Upon a hundred leagues of floor
With her light heels and mocking
Percy and Douglas dead
And Bruce on his burial bed,
Where he lies white as may
With wars and leprosy,
And all the kings before
This land was kingless
And all the singers before
This land was songless,
This land that with its dead and living waits the
    Judgement Day.
But they, the powerless dead,
Listening can hear no more
Than a hard tapping on the sounding floor
A little overhead
Of common heels that do not know
Whence they come or where they go
And are content
With their poor frozen life and shallow banishment.

CHAPTER II

THE SOUTH

I LEFT Edinburgh on a bright July Sunday in a 1921 Standard car. It had been given to me for nothing by an old friend, with the guarantee that if it could be made to start it would keep going. Its age and appearance excited a good deal of interest at the petrol stations where I stopped, but I found it skittered along the roads quite briskly, except for a trick of dancing like a high-spirited colt when I forced it to over thirty-five miles an hour. At a steady thirty it produced a calm, loud snore, which had a pleasantly lulling effect in the windless bright weather. After I had run south for an hour the car got so heated that I had to cast off everything I wore except my shirt and trousers, the best and most comfortable clothing, I found, for travelling in summer.

I took the main South Road, for I wished to spend the night in Jedburgh, stopping at Galashiels, Melrose and Dryburgh on the way: an easy run. I passed field after field of young green corn, amid which multitudes of poppies flaunted with an Arabian brilliance in the bright weather. I saw signposts bearing such names as Dunbar and Haddington, and passed many bare grey farmsteads and an occasional ruined castle.

After a while the fields grew thinner and faded away, giving place to green hills dotted with sheep, and presently I found myself in the Gala Valley, running along the Gala Water. This countryside south of Edinburgh has a business-like plainness and fertility: the poppies, indeed, are a chance embellishment, almost an intrusion; but the exquisite gradation of greens in the fields and the hills belong by right to this landscape. It is both very plain and very vivid, without any ornament except of colour, and that confined to several shades of green; but these run through such an astonishingly various scale, and are all, even the softest, so brilliant, that they produce a strangely light and exhilarating feeling. As I ran down towards Galashiels the green became more and more tinged with brown as the hills grew higher, but when Galashiels came in sight the hills sank again and the green returned, as bright and jewel-like as ever.

In Galashiels the streets were all red and blue with bunting. By a man at the garage where I parked my car I was told that on the previous day the town had held its great annual festival, when the young people had ridden the marches and crossed the Tweed, returning again in the evening.

I turned into a little restaurant, where I was given excellent stew and milk pudding. A great rank of charabancs was standing outside in a square, with the names of all the famous towns and shrines in the Tweed Valley displayed on their fronts. Although it was Sunday the town was swarming with tourists and holiday-makers. The townspeople themselves were in a state of gradually subsiding excitement after their festival, and loud peals of female laughter kept coming from the other public room of the restaurant whenever the door swung open. The streets were so neat and clean, and showed so few of the signs which usually follow a festival, that I could scarcely believe anything had happened. The waitress advised me to go and see the Market Cross, which, she said, was most beautifully decked with flowers. I climbed a steep street to the old town, and found the cross at a bleak corner; but the flowers had wilted, and they were theologically bullied into a joyless pattern. A few old women were standing about sadly admiring them.

Galashiels is a typical border town, clean, bright, and with a stir in its atmosphere which tells that it has a life of its own. The streets are low and broad; there is a satisfying amount of room in the centre of the place, where the Gala Water, artificially compressed within a stony gulley, foams over a miniature fall. Round green hills rise on every side, and in certain of the streets one can see them over the low roofs, when they look much nearer than they actually are. These hills, with the cattle grazing on them, give the town an appearance of having been dropped complete into a pastoral landscape, where it pursues a life at once cut off and autonomous. One gets a somewhat similar impression from the little towns which decorate medieval and early Renaissance Flemish landscapes.

These little border towns, such as Galashiels, Kelso,

Selkirk and Hawick, have all this curiously wakeful and vivid air. I say "curiously," for most of the other small towns I have seen in Scotland are contentedly or morosely lethargic, sunk in a fatalistic dullness broken only by scandal-mongering and such alarums as drinking produces; a dead silence punctuated by malicious whispers and hiccups. But the border towns have kept their old traditions more or less intact, and wherever that happens it is a sign that the common life is still vigorous. In places like Montrose and Kirriemuir there is none of this vigorous public life, and no common object or event except the feats of the local football team in which everybody has a share. The sole claim to eminence of the old resident there is that he knows everything about the private lives of his townsmen; and so devoid are such places of any other interest that this claim is publicly acknowledged to be a justified source of pride. The window in Thrums which Sir James Barrie fitted so skilfully with stained glass is really, in its unendowed state, a horrific symbol of small-town Scottish life: there is nothing one feels, after listening to Thrums gossip in any place, that cannot be seen and is not seen through these destructive panes. The life of these towns, from top to bottom, is merely an aggregate of private lives under a microscope: private lives carried on with the greatest difficulty, forced indeed to become fantastically private beneath a reciprocal and insatiable scrutiny. This window with which the houses in the small towns of Scotland are fitted has the power both to enlarge and diminish everything that is seen through it; bad deeds swell and good deeds shrink; for its peculiar power is that of reducing everything to the same common measure. Such a mode of existence is the expression of a frustration so deep that, while being revolted by it, one cannot help feeling sorry for those who endure it. Something resembling it can doubtless be found in any English small town; but the Scots are more thorough than the English, especially in small things, and it is this thoroughness which makes life in a Scottish small town so insect-like. This uniform chronicle of smallness is broken at rare intervals by some violent episode, when a black sheep of the flock goes resoundingly to the devil. But even such portents are quickly reduced to proportion by the indispensable window, and the reign of law is again vindicated.

In the border towns one does not feel this constricting atmosphere, and it is because they have an active life of their own. They had not broken with their past like Montrose and Kirriemuir, leaving nothing but a vacuum; they have an industry, the weaving of tweeds and other woollen cloths, which, being essentially local and distinctive, has survived the intensifying onset of Industrialism that has eaten into the core of other communities. Perhaps, too, their geographical position, the fact that for centuries they existed almost on the frontier of a hostile foreign nation, strengthened their individuality as units, and impressed upon them so strongly the need for united

effort, yet it has not disappeared. The essential
virtues of a nation generally gather at their greatest
strength not at its centre but at the places where it
is most powerfully and persistently threatened: its
frontiers. The Border formed a rampart against
English invasion for centuries, and it is still the part
of Scotland which is least Anglicised. As soon as one
is within sound of the Tweed one can feel the
presence of history, in the landscape and in the faces
and manners of the people. Over the rest of Scotland
one has to dig for history beneath a layer of débris left
by the Reformation and the Industrial Revolution.

The history of the Borders has accordingly a greater
feeling of depth than that of the rest of the Lowlands.
In Edinburgh, St. Andrews, Linlithgow and Dunkeld
there are churches and houses—the former mostly
ruins—which belong to the old Catholic Scotland; but
one cannot help feeling that the effective history of
the towns themselves began with the Reformation,
that their historical roots are shallow and modern.
These old buildings have the interest merely of
antiquities; they are becalmed in a past that is quite
dead. But in the Borders one feels that history goes
back without a break to the time of Bruce and is continued beyond that in legend. The Reformation certainly reached out and absorbed the Borders in due
time; but the absorption was never so complete as in
the rest of the Lowlands, for the genius of the Border
people was already too completely formed to be funda-
mentally altered. That genius was partly heroic and

partly poetical, and its most essential expression is the ballads, which form the greatest body of Catholic poetry in Scottish literature, greater even than that of Henryson and Dunbar. These ballads continued to be sung and written long after the Reformation without any fundamental change of spirit, so that it is easy now to mistake an eighteenth-century ballad for a sixteenth-century one. In calling the ballads Catholic I am using that term very loosely, and mean by it nothing more than that the ballads possess a quality which the rest of Scottish poetry after the Reformation lacks. Burns is a very Protestant poet. Even in his remoulding of old folk songs he never goes back in sentiment past the Reformation. He certainly had no affection for the God of Knox, yet he himself had no other, except on occasion an eighteenth-century abstraction. His ribaldry, blasphemy, libertinism and sentimentality are all Protestant, and quite narrowly so. The ballads are without this local Lowland Scots limitation. In their view of life they are older than Protestantism; and it is this depth of inspiration which is their distinctive quality. They are like a wedge of solid life going back through all the vicissitudes of Scottish history, an unchanging pattern of the Scottish spirit as it was before Protestant theology, and James VI's long visit to London, and the bribery and corruption of 1704, and industrial progress had changed it in such a strange and inevitable way. The normal development of a nation is a development founded solidly on its past. The development of Scotland during the last three centuries has been a development bought at the expense of shedding one bit of its past after another, until almost the only thing that remains now is a sentimental legend. But I shall touch on this later.

Melrose Abbey lies on the opposite side of the Tweed from Galashiels, at a distance of a few miles. The houses of the pleasant little town have washed up until they almost enclose these ruins. At certain intervals between the successive English invasions the church must have been a lovely edifice; it is now, after being wrecked again and again, and neglected over long periods, indescribably pathetic. The abbey was first founded in 1136 by David I to take the place of an ancient Culdee one in Old Melrose. It lay in the direct road of the English invaders, and was despoiled again and again. Bruce restored it in 1326, but it was once more laid waste in 1385. Towards the end of the fifteenth century it was rebuilt, but the Earl of Hertford wrecked it yet again in 1544 and 1545, and after that it did not recover. The Reformers themselves do not seem to have "purified" it very drastically, that is, broken its images and stolen its treasures; but neglect was in the long run equally deadly, and the ruins were for a long time used as a quarry by local house-builders. These peaceful vandals, along with five centuries of changing weather, have probably done more harm to the abbey than Calvinism and invasion combined; the west front and the west end of the nave have vanished; and a great part of the complete edifice is now a tranquil design drawn on beautiful old sward. A slender, pointed window, still by a miracle intact, faces one as one enters; the broken shafts in the roofless South aisle are of an exquisite lightness and grace, which their mutilation only emphasises. It is hard to say what makes Melrose Abbey so melancholy; the remains of the fine cathedral at St. Andrews awaken a far colder response. Perhaps it is a sense of the number of times that Melrose Abbey has been destroyed; perhaps it is the great window rising beyond the line of splintered shafts as one enters. At any rate, one cannot look at it still without feeling that with it something of transcendent loveliness passed from the life of Scotland, and something which was quite real to the people who came there once. That, whatever it was, was greater than any memorial that has survived of the life of the Borders; greater even than the Ballads. It is a pity that this should be confused with the name of Walter Scott. The ubiquity of Scott's presence in the Borders a hundred years after his death, the persistence with which he has set his mark on the landscape, as if he were resolved to be a Border laird and extort the homage of one in perpetuity, is exasperating. Tom Purdie, his favourite servant, and Peter Matheson, his coachman, are buried in the graveyard adjoining Melrose Abbey. And he himself lies in St. Mary's Aisle in Dryburgh Abbey, with Lockhart, appropriately enough, at his feet.

On the road from Melrose to Dryburgh I reached, after a stiff climb, the point still called "Sir Walter's

View." Here Scott always stopped his horse when he
was returning from his many excursions in the east
country, and here, the legend runs, it stopped of itself
as it returned after its master's burial at Dryburgh.
From this corner Abbotsford can be seen several miles
away, lying in its little green valley beside the Tweed,
and beyond it abrupt low hills, following the course
of the river, roll to the western sky. To the south,
almost immediately opposite, rise the three strange
cone-like summits of the Eildon Hills, within whose
valleys Thomas the Rhymer is said to have spent three
years with the Queen of the Fairies. This landscape
which Scott loved so much is not grand or savage like
some of the Highlands, but has a curious enchantment, the intimate magic of toy scenery invented by
a child. These hills, so large in design and so small
in scale, seem to be formed to be the home of fairies
and gnomes; and the legends which have gathered
round them are a real expression of the natural quality
they possess. The Eildons, it is said, were once one
hill, but it was split into three in a single night by
a demon acting at Michael Scot's bidding. One cannot look at them still without the feeling that something very strange once happened to them and that
they are the result of some inexplicable geological
vicissitude, of which the legend is merely an imaginative expression. It is from this curious landscape that
Scott must have drawn the inspiration for his most
beautiful poem, "Proud Maisie." It is not quite a
human landscape, yet it is not in the least frightening:

its strangeness is like the strangeness of a magical charm which is also harmless.

When one enters Dryburgh Abbey one leaves this curious country behind and is back in ordinary time again. The position of this beautiful ruin in a little loop of the Tweed is the most charming thing about it. Like Melrose it was again and again despoiled by the English, and the Earl of Hertford, who seems to have had a spite against Scottish architecture, was its final murderer. It has decayed more contentedly than Melrose into the status of a ruin. The cloister garth, a little sunken square of exquisite turf, is the core of its strange and perhaps meaningless peace. One queer sight may be seen at Dryburgh. It is the hereditary burial ground of the Haigs of Bemersyde, a family of whom Thomas the Rhymer once prophesied:

> "Tyde what may betyde
> Haig shall be Haig of Bemersyde."

I found the sward on the grave of the late Lord Haig dotted with calico poppies, which were stuck into the turf with long black pins. This is the sole modern touch in this shrine.

The journey from Dryburgh to Jedburgh is through plain and fertile agricultural country. I reached the town in the afternoon under a hot sun which seemed to have driven all the people from the Sunday streets. Having found a hotel I took a bath and went down to the bar-parlour, where two motor-bus drivers were sitting at tea, talking to the landlord. They were returning with an excursion party which they had driven all the way from the Midlands to Skye and half-way back again, a job which had kept them at their posts from early morning until late in the evening. The landlord told me that they were old friends of his and had stopped at his hotel for the last ten years whenever they passed through. They spoke of an accident which had happened to a bus belonging to a different firm a few days before. The bus had been rushing down a hill at a great speed with the engine off (to save petrol), and had banged straight into a small car slowly going in the same direction, carrying it along for thirty yards before the brakes could be applied. They talked about this incident as they might have talked about any other piece of news, but with a seriousness behind which apprehension was hidden; and when I asked—not without anxiety either, for one doesn't like to hear of such incidents when one is setting out on a motor tour—what had happened to the driver of the car, there was a perceptible pause before they replied, and they looked at me suspiciously, as if there were some concealed and possibly unfriendly meaning behind my words. Presently they got up, saying: "Well, we must get back," bade the landlord a cordial good-bye, and stamped out. They were Northumberland men, and I realised that for them the frontier was still there, and that they were in a foreign country. From their comportment they might have been two cattle-drovers stopping at a Border change-house two hundred years ago.

After having had a glass of beer and a sandwich I went out to look at the town. The abbey, a fine up-standing building of red sandstone overlooking the little stream which flows past the town, the Jed, is in a much better state of preservation than Melrose or Dryburgh. Its fate was the same as the other Border buildings, culminating in the inevitable appearance of the Earl of Hertford. The church must have been at one time a proud and well-set-up building, the public centre of the town, and it is without the secluded and rustic charm of Melrose and Dryburgh. It can be seen for miles around, set in a well-defined eminence half way up the hill over which the little town sprawls. There is a lovely wheel window on the west front, and the long nave has three tiers of fine light arches. Outside the churchyard wall runs a charming broad walk raised several feet above the street, with occasional benches where one can sit as on a platform and watch the Sunday evening promenaders passing by. The houses surrounding the abbey are not ancient, but they are built in the traditional Scottish style and do not offend the eye.

The highest point in the town is still called the castle, but the castle was many years ago replaced by a jail, an ugly, low, castellated building which looks like a squat crown set on the charming little place. In the street leading up to it are many handsome houses of rough stone, which have somewhat fallen from their former grandeur, but still look well, except the ones that are smeared with a plastering of lime, a genteel custom which destroys their character and gives them a trumpery, harlotish look.

When I returned after a cursory glance at the prison I found a Salvation Army meeting in full blast in the market square. A young Cockney was testifying with great ingenuousness to the joy that Christ had brought into his life, while about fifteen yards away, at the farthest corner of the square, five or six Border youths were pretending not to listen. The houses round the square seemed to be quite empty; every ten minutes or so a solitary pedestrian would pass, his eyes fixed in front as if the little ring of Salvationists were in a different world; the cobbles, the house walls, the clear space of sky above, seemed to echo with vacancy. I took up my station at another corner. The young Cockney went on addressing nothing without any sign of discouragement, telling it of the great change in his life, and pleading with it to come to Christ. But when at last, with a final protestation of his goodwill to it, he seized his concertina and rollicked into a cheery hymn, he could not keep a look of desperation from flitting over his face. But after that he immediately resumed the expression of simple and frank concern for the salvation of his imaginary hearers which was obviously the true reflection of his feelings.

I waited on after he had stopped, for the spectacle of a simple Cockney youth wrestling with the complicated puzzle of Scottish insensibility was extraordinarily touching. The Cockney was superseded, somewhat patronisingly, by an older Salvationist, who by his accent belonged to the Midlands and was an experienced gatherer of the souls of trade-unionists. His argument for surrender to Christ was as full of topical points as a sermon preached by a Nonconformist parson who keeps up with the *British Weekly;* he touched on unemployment, Socialism, pacifism, the class war, the state of things in Germany, even football, the last refuge of the broad-minded evangelist; but at last he too had resignedly to give out a hymn, and the little band of men, women and children marched away to their hall, into which they had managed to lure not one follower. There, for the rest of the evening, I could hear them singing as I walked about the quiet streets; a forlorn and yet business-like sound. While the meeting in the square was going on I had felt sorry for a boy of ten who kept looking about shamefacedly while his mother in her blue uniform held him firmly by the hand. Anybody could see that he was not listening to the message of salvation. Probably he was thinking of the chaff he would have to stand next day from his schoolmates.

After the Salvationists had left I took a walk through the streets in the clear evening light. There was hardly anybody about, and the town was silent except for the distant singing coming from the Salvation Army Hall. The houses looked empty, and I could have imagined that they really were if I had not seen now and then a woman or a girl sitting motionless at a window. Behind these transparent barriers they looked very near and yet very remote, like mermaids in an aquarium, or waxwork princesses waiting for bucolic rescuers, and I felt that the empty streets on which they looked out were just as remote and strange to them. They did not seem to be watching for anything, like the housewives of Thrums; and indeed there was nothing to be seen but the empty streets and the light still lingering on the small green hills outside the town.

The long narrow closes which open off the main street are charming. It is surprising that modern towns are not built more in this style, for even if the main thoroughfare were roaring with traffic in Jedburgh, one could in a moment find seclusion and silence in these little retreats. They are just too narrow for a vehicle of any kind to enter, a precious advantage in modern towns; and at the backs of the houses are gardens completely enclosed and sheltered. I do not know whether there is any irrevocable architectural objection to this style of town-planning, which so mathematically ensures quietness in the midst of the greatest noise; but it seemed to me a simple solution of a disagreeable problem. There are many of these little closes running from the main street in Jedburgh to The Friars, a charming back street, on whose other side rises an abrupt green hill with big houses and flowering gardens.

As I returned to my hotel I passed a crowd of dwarf-like youths who were clearly foreign to the place, for they walked with that strut which is one of the gifts bequeathed to us by American films. While I was at supper the waitress told me that a silk mill had been recently set up in the place, since which there had been no unemployment; indeed a number of people had had to be brought into the town from outside. These youths were obviously among the invaders, for they had the defiant self-consciousness of a different race and, I noticed, stuck close together. They looked tiny and elegant compared with the tall, hefty natives of the town; but their narrow waists and challenging strut gave them the formidable appearance of gunmen out for a walk which might not end harmlessly. They were no doubt ordinary factory workers, but in the setting of Jedburgh they produced that impression of illicit, almost criminal knowledge which makes the factory hands of the towns so strange, so alluring and yet so repellent to people unaccustomed to industrial life. It was strange to see these young men there.

The mill worked all the time, the waitress went on, and that explained an undercurrent of sound which I had occasionally felt through the Sunday peace. When I went up to my bedroom I could see the twin-stacks of the silk factory through the window: one of them red and clean, the other black with smoke, both like thin pencils. Below, in the yard of the inn, five or six kittens were playing round an empty packing case. Over the roofs of the town the gable of a house standing on a hill shone red among green trees; the chimney pots were a glowing rose colour in the level light. The fields, dotted with trees and sheep, looked very close and bright, and by the time the radiance had died away it was late, the town was asleep, and only the tremor of sound from the silk-works faintly disturbed the silence.

Next morning the streets had come alive; buses were starting in the square when I got up; and a cool breeze had risen. My first call was Abbotsford, which is shut on Sundays; and to reach it I had to retrace a part of the road I had taken. A bus was standing at the gate of Abbotsford when I arrived and a large party was being shown round. I paid for my ticket and joined it.

Abbotsford is a very strange house. It is a place certainly well-suited to be displayed, to astonish, to stagger, and to sadden; but that it should ever have been lived in is the most astonishing, staggering, saddening thing of all. One feels, while wandering through it, that one is on the track of a secret more intimate than either Scott's biography or his written works can tell; and that if one stayed here long enough one would at last understand the mania which drove him to create this pompous, crude, fantastic, unmanageable, heartless, insatiable, comfortless brute of a house, and sacrifice to it in turn his genius, his peace of mind, his health and his life. Everything in it, except the study with its secret stair, where Scott slipped down in the early morning to write his romances unknown to his guests, is designed for ostentation; it is a huge showroom of vulgar romantic properties. The library, a long wide hall with high windows looking down on the Tweed, is like a public library. The house itself, with its persistently repeated turrets, might be a railway hotel designed in the baronial style. In this barracks antique swords, armorial bearings, ancient suits of mail, dungeon keys, and all kinds of rusty lumber meet one at every turn. Archbishop Sharp's fire-grate and Balfour of Burley's snuff-box; the pulpit of the old kirk of Dunfermline and the door of the old Tolbooth Prison; Burns's toddy tumbler and Napoleon's pen and writing-case; a German heading-sword and the crucifix which Mary Stuart bore on her way to execution; Rob Roy's purse, sporran, claymore and dirk; Prince Charlie's quaich; the keys of Selkirk jail and Lochleven Castle; sabres, cutlasses, daggers, pistols, blunderbusses: Scott, it seems, could not have enough of such things, and could swallow the most crude and worthless lumber if it was only sanctified by history. The ceiling of the library is a bad copy of the carvings in Roslin Chapel. The walls of the drawing-room are covered with emerald-green Chinese wall-paper. It shows scenes of Chinese life interwoven with floral scrolls, and near the door Mr. George Bernard Shaw, in a Chinese robe, can be seen talking a century before his time. It is an astonishingly faithful like-ness; easily, indeed, the best I have ever come across.

The study, a smaller, square, high room, is the place in the house which one can most nearly believe in. The desk is enormous, being both high and massive, and makes one realise that Scott was almost a giant. Here, to use his own phrase about Byron, he "wielded his pen with the negligent ease of a man of quality." One imagines him stealing down in the morning before his guests were awake, finishing off a paper duel, changing, and appearing in the dining-room surrounded by his dogs, a Border laird more convincing than nature. A fantastic life in a fantastic house.

To realise how fantastic that life was one has only to look at Raeburn's magnificent portrait which hangs in the Chinese drawing-room. Chantrey's bust in the library, said to be the best likeness of Scott, shows us merely the laird. But Raeburn's portrait is that of a very remarkable man. The fine eyes have a gipsy fire beneath the overhanging brows, but the whole expression is one of passion so firmly suppressed that it seems to darken every feature, giving out smoke instead of flame except through the eyes. The body, leaning forward as if preparing to spring, looks twisted and dwarflike in spite of its bulk, and the arms have a contorted look, as if they were straining against invisible fetters. This broad and twisted body surmounted by the powerful head with its flashing eyes is both menacing and pathetic; expressing simultaneously consciousness of power and of defeat. The face might be that of a lifelong outcast or a lifelong prisoner who has never resigned himself to his lot.

As impressive in another way is the death mask that lies in the turret-room. It shows the face of a man who, after struggling on courageously and drawing on his powers to the end, has found that that is not enough; so that all the features are fixed in painful surprise. The mouth is pulled down like that of a hurt child; but the rest of the face expresses steady offence.

This mask, like Raeburn's portrait, shows passion in every line: offended pride, hurt vanity, defeated ambition, frustrated hope. Abbotsford impresses one as the concrete expression of this passion; for only that can make it comprehensible, and Scott's strong and deadly attachment to it; explaining its fantastic taste- lessness and ostentation, even its comfortlessness. Writers with a strong and reckless love of life, such as Scott and Balzac, often have this omnivorous collect- ing passion; it is an expression of their desire to make life quite their own, to possess and hold it concretely. To do this they will endure the greatest sacrifices, in- volve themselves in lifelong debt, and finally work themselves to death in the service of their appetite. Such a hunger for life has something indecent in it; it will devour anything, from Mary Stuart's head an hour after her execution to a scrap of oatcake found on Culloden Moor; and it will do this with all the circumstances of publicity that it can get; for men gifted or cursed with this appetite for life are forced at last to proclaim it publicly so that they might be freed from its obsession. Balzac's taste was more universal than Scott's, which comprehensively ignored one sphere of life, sensual passion, or else treated it from a genteel distance; and so all the relics that are gathered together at Abbotsford express violent and dramatic masculine action, and are in some way con- nected with battles, forays, assassinations, imprison- ments, escapes, victories, executions. They were assembled there by a mania which would have liked to

find expression in the actual employment of these
weapons of war, but was by necessity compelled to
forgo any more direct use of them than the creation
of an obsolete arsenal and the invention, in a long
series of romances, of a dream of violent and lawless
life. It must have been the "Ivanhoe" side of Scott
that built and furnished Abbotsford. Consequently it
is both real and unreal, like "Ivanhoe," and has the
inspired tastelessness of a substitute which is indispensable. It is surely the saddest and strangest monument that Scott's genius created.

From Abbotsford I made westward for Selkirk, a
bustling little town with statues of Scott and Mungo
Park and a tablet marking an inn where Burns once
lodged. I did not stop, for I wished to reach the valley
of the Yarrow, which begins a few miles beyond the
town, hoping that I might manage to see it with my
own eyes, ignoring the enchantment which legend and
romantic poetry have thrown over it. But that was a
vain hope, for all these things are now a part of Yarrow,
and to-day one can no more erase them than one can
put time back. In themselves the Banks of Yarrow
consist of a number of green grassy slopes, some gentle,
some precipitous, dotted with birches and an occasional
grey ruin among trees. They are enchantingly pretty,
and in them the toy-like character of the Border
scenery is worked out to its last conclusion. The
stream itself produces the effect of a great river, such
as the Danube or the Rhine, done in miniature; the
outline of its banks are bold and various, but tiny in

scale, giving a feeling of great riches gathered into a little span. At the turn where Newark Castle "looks out from Yarrow's birchen bower" all its enchantment can be felt, and gazing down at it from there one can seize simultaneously the two things which give it its character: a wild, tangled prettiness and a tradition of bloodshed. The high narrow banks give protection to a host of wild flowers, as they have done in the past to so many secret encounters.

In its higher reaches the Yarrow flows between low bare hills open to the sky. Lonely farms, rolling heath and anglers' inns appear, and everything looks bleak and cold even on a July day until one reaches St. Mary's Loch. This I found a disappointment after Wordsworth's beautiful lines about the swan floating double, swan and shadow. A cold breeze had suddenly got up, the surface of the loch was covered with ripples, and the hills running down to it looked shrunken and mean. I lunched at Tabbie Shiel's Inn, a little anglers' hotel where Christopher North and James Hogg once passed a hilarious evening and many of the famous men of that period, including De Quincey, Aytoun and Lockhart, put in. It is a bare little white-washed place with a tasteless modern annex, and in itself extraordinarily empty of atmosphere. But it provided me with an excellent cold lunch.

When one takes the road from St. Mary's Loch west-ward to Moffat one soon finds oneself in a completely different country. The very names have a different ring. One no longer finds the light and musical place names of the Tweed Valley, in which one can hear the tinkle of its streams—Melrose, Galashiels, Fountainhall, Temple, Eildon, Deloraine—but is among comfortable, substantial, beefy names like Beattock, Moffat, Lockerbie, Lochmaben, Dumfries, Annan. As soon as the Yarrow is out of sight behind the last turn of the road the hills become large, plain, green, heavy, grand, prosaic; hills for sheep, shepherds, Bible-readers and a sober peasantry devoted to plain living and high thinking. The vast sides of these mounds are quite smooth, as if they were moulded out of some too soft and slithery material; they look like mud-castles on a gigantic scale over which a good thick padding of fat turf has been drawn, so that although they are apparently solid and immovable they give a feeling of insecurity; for they are smooth as well as steep, and quite treeless; smooth as a crowd of vast and stupid shaven conical heads. One feels one could dig into their fat sides without ever finding a core of rock, nothing but soft, black, moist, sticky soil, without foundation or variation. Little fragments of boulder lie scattered over their thewless sides like minute excretions. These plasticine hills are among the strangest I have ever come across, and I was glad when, as I neared Moffat, woods and ordinary slopes began to appear again.

When one is past Moffat, a pleasant little country town, one begins to penetrate into the rich agricultural county of Dumfriesshire. The soil seems to get deeper and deeper; everywhere signs of fruitfulness press in upon one; and one's mind is insensibly filled with thoughts of live stock, cattle-shows, prize bulls, and Scots love in the Burns style. These fields, one tells oneself, must be well manured. Fertility here is a solid, organised industry. Even the woods have a rank look, as if primitive rites had gone on in them for centuries. Places naturally fertile and organised for fertility, where the bull becomes the communal symbol (as he is in many modern agricultural communities), produce a different conception of love from lighter and more barren regions. The love-songs of Dumfriesshire and the Mearns, another region famed for its fertility in Scotland, are mainly Rabelaisian, and quite unlike those of the Highlands or the Borders. They are completely of the soil, for fertility is as close a shackle as dearth, fettering the peasant not merely by necessity, but by all his senses, until his mind becomes as dull and rich as the landscape on which it feeds. When romantic sentiment does break out, it becomes as lush as the famous lines on Annie Laurie; but the prevailing attitude to love is expressed in ballads which cannot be quoted in a modern book of travel, and in certain songs of Burns. There is a great difference between:

"Come to my arms, my Katie, my Katie,
  Come to my arms and kiss me again.
  Drunken or sober, here's to thee, Katie,
  And blest be the hour that I did it again."

and—

"Like watercress gathered fresh from cool streams,
   Thy kiss, dear love, on the Bens of Jura,"

the former of which is by Burns, and the latter a poor
translation of a Hebridean song which must be lovely
in the original. This poetry is quite without the super-
human passion of the Border love ballads, which
leaps the ordinary bounds of experience and passes
into dream.

"Tak hame your hawks, tak hame your kye,
   For they hae bred our sorrow;
   I wiss that they had a' gane mad,
   When they cam first to Yarrow."

The average range of passion that Lowland poetry
reaches is shown in such verses as:

"But a' the joys the world can gi'e,
   Tho' three times doubled fairly,
   That happy night was worth them a',
   Amang the rigs o' barley."

Yet it is happier at a less exalted level than this.
The Border ballads achieve magic through passion,
the Gaelic songs through some inexplicable refinement of sensibility; but the only two magical lines that
Burns wrote were inspired by a tragic apprehension
of his own fate:

"The wan moon is setting behind the white wave
   And time is setting for me, O."

Dumfriesshire looks to the passer's eye like the classical incarnation of the trinity which Matthew Arnold disliked so much: Scotch drink, Scotch love and Scotch religion. It is solid, fertile and handsome. There may be found in certain districts of it, I have been told, a great number of people who look very like Burns. This fact has never been explained by local historians, as far as I know.

Dumfries itself is a blowsy, overgrown country town of which Maxwelltown, with its braes, has now become a part. I cannot help stopping here to consider the strange popularity of "Annie Laurie," for I feel it is a symbol of modern Scotland. The melody itself has an obvious fascination which might make one sing it twice or thrice, until one discovers that it is mechanical in its rise and fall. As for the poem, it is an almost unique anthology of hackneyed similes. Annie Laurie's brow is like the snow-drift, her neck is like the swan, her face the fairest that ever the sun shone on, the fall of her fairy feet is like dew on the gowan lying, her voice low and sweet as winds in summer sighing, and so on. The only originality of the poem consists in certain errors of observation, no woman's neck being like a swan except by a rhetorical mistake, and the fall of fairy feet being quite unlike dew *lying* on a gowan. Such mistakes of observation are hardly ever found in genuine folk poetry, which is exact and to the point, as, for instance, in the lines:

"Yestreen I made my bed fu' wide,
  Tonight I'll make it narrow,
For a' the sad and leelang night
  I'll lie twined o' my marrow."

The enduring popularity of "Annie Laurie" is a sign
that true folk sentiment in Scotland has for a long time
been degenerating, so that a sham substitute is more
pleasing to Scottish ears than the real thing.

By such a verse as:

"'A bed! A bed!' Clerk Saunders said,
  'A bed for you and me!'
'Fy na! Fy na!' said May Margaret,
  'Till ance we married be,'"

the ordinary Scotsman and Scotswoman nowadays
would feel their sensibilities shocked; though at one
time these lines were quite without offence to anyone.

"Annie Laurie" was really the first great public mile-
stone on Scotland's road to the Kailyard and the window in Thrums, and its popularity showed that that
road was predestined. Two things mainly contributed
to set Scotland, an eminently realistic country, on such
a path: the breakdown of Calvinism, a process salutary
in itself, but throwing off as a by-product an obliterat-
ing débris of sentimentality, and the rise of an industrial system so sordid and disfiguring that people
were eager to escape from it by any road, however
strange. The flight to the Kailyard was a flight to Scot-

land's past, to a country which had existed before Industrialism; but by the time the flight took place Industrialism itself had sucked that tradition dry of its old vigour; it was no longer of importance except as a refuge from the hard facts of Scottish town life. The Kailyard school of literature was thus really a by-product of Scotland's economic history. All the songs and stories of Scottish country life after the Industrial Revolution got into its stride were for a long time dreams of comfort or escape. To anyone living in Glasgow or Dundee even the Kailyard must have seemed heaven. George Douglas Brown assailed this dream in *The House with the Green Shutters,* and that was the reason why he was attacked with such bitterness. Before the Industrial Revolution the Scottish writer described country scenes vigorously and realistically: there are as scathing domestic interiors in Burns himself, though he marked the deterioration of tradition, as in *The House with the Green Shutters.* It was the increasing bestiality of industrial Scotland that turned the countryside of fiction into a *Schlaraffenland,* and made Scottish literature for a time mainly a literature written by sentimental ministers.

I did not stop in Dumfries, but from a number of men, young and old, standing at the street corners, I could see that it was suffering from unemployment: the first outward sign of that complaint which I had observed since coming to the Borders. But I knew well enough that unemployment must exist, too, in the smaller towns and in the countryside: for the evils of civilisation are obvious only in the towns, and one has to live for some time in the country before one discovers them. Thinking this as I drove past Annie Laurie's braes, now covered with tasteless council houses, I remembered a time when I had lived in a small town in Sussex. The house I stayed in opened on a little country lane, and every morning about ten o'clock I would see a group of young men wandering down it to the Labour Exchange which lay at the foot of the hill. They walked along idly, with the vacant air of people who have no real place to go to or are holding a rendezvous with themselves; and their punctual passing every morning in that country lane with its high hedges brought the universality of unemployment before me more vividly than the street corners of the big industrial towns have ever done since. There was a public recreation-ground a little distance away, and there all summer endless games of cricket were played by these youths and men; they played on, day after day, until they obviously had no interest in the game, and it had become merely a way of filling up a vacuum which to them was the world. They are probably still doing the same thing this summer, and may be doing it ten years hence. When I walked out a little distance from the town and saw the farm labourers working in the fields, doing tasks which had been done for centuries, I sometimes felt that it was they who were playing on in a world that had stopped, they who were the anomaly, while these young men wandering down to the Labour Exchange (by then a merely ironical term) represented the authentic reality of the modern world. But I did not see enough of rustic Scotland, except in the very north, in the Orkney Islands, where things are quite different, to become aware of this aspect of it, which I came to know so well in Sussex. Dumfriesshire certainly has a prosperous look, for its fields are fertile and rich, whatever may be the condition of its peasantry.

The whole appearance of the landscape changed as I reached Kirkcudbrightshire. Dumfriesshire is mainly rolling country, mounting and falling in wide, easy sweeps. But in Kirkcudbrightshire the ground is delicately varied, and the small abrupt hills are broken up into little terraced shelves of green. This interruption of all the contours arrests the eye perpetually; there are no grand effects; everything is plain and exquisite. The trees are not massed in thick woods as in Dumfriesshire, but distributed singly or in little clumps, as in a free and open design. So just and classical are the natural contours that a group of cows planted on an abrupt green hill seemed, as I looked, to improvise a sort of rustic Acropolis and Parthenon all complete. It was late afternoon when I passed through this country on my way to Kirkcudbright. I drove slowly; the air was sunny and clear, so that I could see, beyond the tossing hills of Kirkcudbrightshire, all bright green, the dark mountains of Galloway, which in that landscape had a menacing, intrusive look. Kirkcudbrightshire is certainly one of the most beautiful counties in Scotland, and one of the most unspoilt. Its scenery has something of the toy-like charm of the Tweed and Yarrow country; but it evokes no memories or associations, and appeals to one purely by the endless variety of its shapes. The soil is far barer and, I fancy, less fertile than that of Dumfriesshire; there are a great number of green fields, all of them uneven; no flatness or regularity, nothing to suggest that the ground has been completely subdued to utilitarian ends, as it is in Dumfriesshire, and become a mere producer of crops. To the rich crop-producing lands one should feel grateful; but there is a point at which they lose their individuality and nature seems to die a little death in them. They produce what man wants them to produce, but perhaps at the expense of refusing him something else. There may be such a thing as pathological over-fertility; at any rate, I feel that there is an ideal balance between the soil and man who lives on it, that the ground itself has certain rights, and that when these are violated the relation between man and nature goes wrong. This may be a fancy, but I think that it exists as a quite genuine conviction in ordinary people who live in immediate contact with the soil, in small farmers, for example, to whom ploughing and reaping are more than a business.

I reached Kirkcudbright, hot and covered with dust. I stopped at the first hotel I saw and asked if I could have a room for the night. The hotel proprietor first gave me a look, then went to the door, gave a look at the car too, seemed to hesitate for a moment, but then said yes, I could have a room. I took a bath and changed and went for a walk through the town, calling in on my way at a chemist's shop, for my face was bursting with heat, and the backs of my hands were beginning to swell where the sun had beat down upon them steadily all day as they rested on the driving-wheel. By the time that the chemist had given me all the advice he could think of for treating sunburn, and sold me a preparation specially made up, he had to shut up his shop and I to return to my hotel for dinner.

It was in the hotel in Kirkcudbright that I first came upon the vanguard of the long procession of English tourists who kept up with me during all my road to the north of Scotland. I have a great admiration for the English people, who are a most highly civilised race; but when they are in a foreign country some of them have a strange and exasperating habit of filling it with the local atmosphere of some provincial or suburban district of their own land. When they appear in a foreign hotel or public room, it is as if they were preceded by an invisible vacuum-cleaner which removes all trace of local associations, so that they may comfortably settle in with the customary aura of their existence quite complete and inviolate round them like a vast immaterial cushion. So I found Maidenhead all round me in Dunkeld, Brixton in Ullapool, and Tunbridge Wells in Scourie. It is not merely that English people of this kind carry England about with them, as a Frenchman carries France; they carry about the street they live in, their back gardens, the views from their windows, their local politics, the churches and shops they patronise, their private jokes, everything that makes them a part of a specific locality. It is as if, from an impulse of self-preservation, they must emphasise all their local characteristics as soon as they find themselves outside their own country. Dunkeld is very unlike Maidenhead, and Ullapool has no resemblance to Brixton, but the more distant the relevance of their actions the more jealously do such people insist on asserting their local standards. This is very strange behaviour, and would be liable to misunderstanding by the natives of Dunkeld and Ullapool if they were not convinced that the English are quite incomprehensible. I do not pretend to understand it: but it seems to me to come from that deep instinct for security which is an essential part of the English character. By behaving as if they were still in Maidenhead or Brixton they abolish the strangeness, possibly hostile, of the places they have temporarily decided to live in. Whatever its causes, this curious phenomenon persistently pursued me in my journey through Scotland.

The vanguard arrived during my dinner at the hotel. I had the dining-room to myself at first; presently two painters, a man and a woman, came in, and began discussing Venice, the Louvre, and other things that interested them. Then the vanguard appeared, a whole tableful, five young men and three ladies slightly older, and the room was immediately filled with an extraordinarily intense atmosphere of suburban elation. I have no idea what suburb the company belonged to, though it was obviously one on distant speaking terms with Bohemia, like so many suburbs. One of the ladies, dark and somewhat plump, had an extraordinarily deep and resonant and yet deliberate laugh which she released in three consecutive peals with a slight interval between, as if she were carefully letting fall three melodious bricks. The young men clamorously called for beer, and while waiting for it compared car speeds. One of the ladies said something about "the girl with the waggling hips," and a young man gravely corrected her: "Excuse me, you mean the damsel with the shuffling buttocks." I was wondering who they were, as the Shufflebottom joke went its round and the dark lady dropped her bricks, when I suddenly saw that the waitress, a simple Calvinistic girl unused to this kind of talk, was looking at me in indignant admonition, and silently ordering me to intervene as a Scotsman in the cause of decency. I weakly looked away, and the rest of my dinner was set down before me in silence. It was a little clash of temperament which must be repeated a hundred times every summer in the hotels of Scotland; quite unimportant and quite silly; but showing the incompatibility between the two peoples, as well as their complementary faults. For the amusing thing, which must have been peculiarly exasperating to the waitress, was that the Shufflebottoms were quite unconscious that anything was wrong.

After dinner I went for a walk through the town. It has a great number of handsome houses, which I believe have been looked after and preserved by the colony of painters who are settled in the town. Most of the houses round the harbour square and in the streets leading off it are painted in various colours, black, dark blue, Payne's grey, yellow—a pleasant surprise in a Scottish street. The harbour square itself is unexpectedly spacious; at one corner, on the banks of the river, stand the dark red ruins of the castle, and close beside them rises a green mound of ancient turf where, as I watched, children were playing, their clear voices carrying far through the evening air. The River Dee has a somewhat sluggish and muddy look where it passes Kirkcudbright, but the low fields adjoining it are enchantingly rich and green. I followed the back street which leads down-stream from the castle, and found many quaint and charming houses and a fat strong gipsy-like young woman in beach pyjamas who was swearing volubly at a little pale-faced boy, probably her son or step-son, who was crouching on the steps of a house. All the acrid and devastating energy of the Scottish character seemed to be in the harridan's voice; her words were like actual missiles shot from her mouth, for the wretched boy jerked and trembled perpetually under them. Yet I doubt whether there was hatred or even anger in them; they had an almost objective sound, as if they were a mere discharge of energy, enjoyable in itself, and without colour or inflection. The sound of them brought back to me many an hour in Glasgow, where long before I had suffered in a less disagreeable way from the distorted, incessant and yet purposeless energy broadcast by the people I met. It was as if they were under a perpetual com-

75

pulsion to assert themselves, and as if they existed only in that assertion. There is just as valid an economic explanation for this as there is for Kailyardism; but I shall come to that later.

The young woman suddenly stopped in the middle of her tirade to throw a joke at two women who were standing non-committally at their doors. A general conversation followed, the boy sat up and listened, and I continued on my way. Presently I found myself at a gate leading into a field adjoining the river, and asked two men, who were also dark and gipsy-like like the woman, and by their appearance seemed to be fishermen, if the path would take me down to the sea. They stopped their conversation and looked at me for a minute, then one of them said in a reluctant voice: "Ay, ye *could* get to the sea that way," his words seeming to imply that there were other and more usual routes. But, having given me an exact answer, he did not seem to think there was any necessity to embroider it with explanations, and turning to his companion resumed his talk. I struck out across the field, keeping to a little footpath. It was after eight; the sky was cloudless and blue; the sun was bright on the lush, wet-looking grass, and lit up brilliantly a line of green hills in the distance; the squat solid trees dotting the field cast long broad shadows. The path wound this way and that, taking me into another field with black cattle and along a ditch filled with meadow-sweet which breathed out a palpable bank of scent into the stagnant air. The place was quite still and deserted, except for the children's cries coming from the harbour square; but they were so near and distinct that I felt for a moment that there could be nothing but children in the town, deserted by their parents. Actually the houses were only a few hundred yards away; but after they have grown up, I reflected, people hardly ever shout except at football matches, and then in unison as if they were afraid of the sound of their separate voices.

I walked along enjoying the silence, and was disappointed when the path brought me back to a point in the main road only a little distance from where I had started. This was the real road to the sea, I found, and I set out on it and walked for two or three miles, after which I learnt that I would have to walk several more if I wanted to reach the coast. But the lower reaches of the Dee were worth the trouble of the walk; the estuary widened and narrowed in the most fascinating way, and I sat for a long time looking at a low odd-shaped island covered with long, coarse, grey-green grass which made it look like the back of some huge furry rodent. Through the last gap between the river-banks I could see the distant, almost impalpable, pale blue mountains of Cumberland.

On my way back to the town I found that grown people shout after all. A girl was running along the side of the road shrieking, pursued by a burly young man with very long gorilla-like arms. She tripped on a grass-blade and fell, like the lady in Boccaccio's story, and the young man fell on the top of her. Presently they got up and repeated the performance. Another couple, who were walking sedately side by side, evidently belonged to the same party: with them was a little girl of seven or eight, asking questions. They were holiday-makers from Glasgow, I discovered, as I passed them. When I got back to the hotel there was great hilarity in the passages. The Shufflebottoms were going to bed.

CHAPTER III

TO GLASGOW

THE scenery of the South-West of Scotland in a line from Kirkcudbright to Girvan is so beautiful and varied that if I were to give all my impressions of it, this chapter would be mainly natural description, and natural description, though a pleasant art, has something of make-believe in it; it pretends to reproduce a scene or a locality, but really expresses the writer's emotions. The day on which I drove from Kirkcudbright to Glasgow was brilliant, hot and windless, and what the scenery I passed through would look like on a day of autumn rain I have not the slightest idea; for weather does not merely change the aspect of nature, but also determines the mood in which we contemplate it. My troubles with the car, which began on this day, did not affect my seeing eye at all, I think; and when, as I came near Girvan, the brakes went on fire, I simply stopped by the side of the road, climbed into a wood, and smoked till they cooled down again. But the sky was so clear, the sun so bright and hot, that all that day seems to me now almost like a dream, a dream of enchantment until I reached Ayr, and something like a nightmare afterwards; for blazing heat and light seem to intensify all one's impressions, making

79

them more delightful if they are delightful, and more painful if they are painful. So if my account of this part of my journey should sound vague, or even be inexact on certain points, I hope the reader will put the blame on one of the hottest days I have ever known.

The first part of my journey was through the broken green country of Kirkcudbrightshire, which by now looked familiar. After Gatehouse of Fleet, a pleasant little secluded town with holiday-makers wandering about the streets, the road ran along the coast of Wigtown Bay. For a time the little green hills accompanied me, but presently the coast-line sank and they along with it; the cliffs and caves fell behind; and as I neared Creetown everything became flat, the shore shrinking to an expanse of mud-coloured sand; and the coast of Wigtownshire opposite, low and drab even in the clear light, did not seem attractive. I did not stop at Creetown, which the guide-book informed me was the Portnaferry in *Guy Mannering*, for I did not want to lose my remaining illusions about that novel, the first of Scott's that I ever read. The little town had the untidy, draggled appearance of most small Scottish towns of a respectable age, except for those in the Tweed Valley: the look of an old crone of settled habits who morosely snuffs and smokes by the chimney-corner. A few miles farther on I came to Newton Stewart, a very charming town with a pleasant stream, the River Cree, flowing past it; the fact that it has a market-day and is the centre of the farm life round it seems to have kept it clean and handsome.

Climbing out of it by a steep road, I suddenly found myself in a landscape quite different from any that I had seen till now. It is difficult to give any impression of that beautiful and almost quite solitary stretch of moorland which lies between Newton Stewart and the bleak village of Barrhill in the south of Ayrshire. For about twenty miles I can remember seeing only two houses. On every side the moorland flowed away in low waves to the horizon, except where it was broken, far away in the east, by the dark mountains of Galloway. There was no sign of life, except for a few distant sheep nibbling the harsh tufts of grass that grew here and there among the heather; even birds did not seem to come here, and the only sound I heard was of one lark singing far up. The thin air was sweetened by a thousand scents rising into it from every tuft in these miles of moorland, mingling as they rose, so that one seemed to be breathing in the landscape itself, drinking it in with all one's senses except that of hearing, which was magically stilled. The silence of such places is so complete that it sinks into one's mind in waves, making it clearer and clearer, drenching it as with a potion concocted out of some positive life-giving essence, not out of the mere absence of sound. In that silence the moor was a living thing spreading its fleece of purple and brown and green to the sun. As I sat in the heather, breathing in the perfume, it seemed to me that I could feel new potentialities of nature working in this scene, secrets that I had never known or else had quite forgotten: perhaps they were merely memories of childhood, when one is capable of being alone with nature as one can rarely be in later years, and is more clearly aware of its powers. There was not one contour, one variation of colour which did not suggest peace and gladness; and the loneliness and silence surrounding the moor were like a double dream enclosing it and making it safe, one might have thought, for ever.

It is from such scenes as this that some Scotsmen I have met, shepherds and workers on remote farms, take the gravity and beauty of their character. Many years ago I met one of them whom I shall never forget, an old shepherd who encouraged me to talk of my life in Glasgow, where he had never been, and spoke of his own approaching death with the composure of one who for many years has contemplated it and looked beyond it. I could see that my youth seemed pathetic to him, and I felt grateful to him for showing interest in something so remote; his interest seemed a kind of magnanimous concession; I can see now that it was probably a distraction of which he was glad. Men of that kind, from whatever land they may come, are a credit to human nature. At one time they were not uncommon in Scotland; Wordsworth knew of them and praised them; but they are rapidly disappearing and have now almost vanished. They are not a poetical or idyllic fancy; I have met them both in the south and the north of Scotland. They are disappearing because the conditions which produced them, solitude and silence, are more and more hard to find. I had stopped my car a little distance past the first house I saw on my journey over the moor. There was no other house in sight, and I was thinking of the complete solitude of the people who lived there, when on looking more closely I saw a motor-car standing in the yard. Loneliness is a condition for the fostering of certain human virtues, and the tendency of modern civilisation is to destroy it indiscriminately. So it is probable that there will soon be none of those Scotsmen left whom Wordsworth admired so much. I merely note this: it would be foolish to lament a change that is inevitable.

I stopped several times on my way across the moor, once on a little rising, and once beside a small loch whose waters were such an intense blue that they seemed to burn spirituously as they rippled in the sun. The village of Barrhill, a waste, squalid place consisting of one wide street of ugly red houses open to all the winds, announced the approach of agricultural land. From there to the pretty little village of Pinwherry I slid down between ordinary fields. But beyond Pinwherry the road led up and down through fine hilly wooded country, and mounting a rise I saw stretched out beneath me a great expanse of flat land with the long narrow huddle of Girvan sprawled over it, and beyond that the sands, the sea, and far out the blank red cone of Ailsa Craig. Coming so recently from the moorlands, I seemed all at once to have before me far too many things for my eyes to take in, and I could not make out at first what the crowd of tiny louse-like forms could be that were crawling over the broad, soiled, mud-coloured sands, until I realised that they must be bathers. From that height and distance, where these shapes were only by inference human, they presented a strangely sad and ignominious spectacle, and the simultaneous knowledge that I was looking at human flesh, yards and yards of human flesh assembled there as by some meaningless feat of mass-production, was such a shock that I hastily started the car again so as to reach the shore and see for myself that these were human beings. They were, I found to my relief. But the sand looked as dirty near at hand as it had looked from the distance, like a huge bed that had been slept on for a long time without the sheets being changed. The sand that stretches beneath most of the holiday resorts along the West of Scotland is only sand by courtesy; that is, it can be made into castles and is soft under one's feet. But it has little resemblance to the fine sand that one finds on remote coasts, and has shrunk into a merely utilitarian convenience, a mass-production of the waves.

I had been in Girvan for a summer holiday once before, and had nearly lost my life there once by getting out of my depth before having learned to swim. This may have helped me to decide that it is a bleak little place, unlike most Scottish sea resorts. But it has not the positive hideousness of such recent growths as Prestwick, of which I shall say something later on. The town did not seem to have changed very much, except for the throngs of buses and cars, and the noise. I resisted the temptation to go in for a swim, remembering this sea's former unkindness, and drove on till I came to a side road leading to a little village where when I was seventeen I had once worked for a few months as sucking chauffeur at a big house: a job I took on because my health had broken down. The country-side seemed unfamiliar and much nakeder than I had remembered, and I passed the lodge of the house where I had worked before I saw it. The village itself, which lay a little farther on over a tiny bridge, was recognisable as a bleached and picked skeleton of itself. My memory had provided the houses in the main street with flourishing gardens, but these were withered now to a little flower strip before one house. The place, which then had seemed full of boisterous life, too full for me, for its boisterousness was one half ill-nature, was quite torpid, and most of the houses showed signs of neglect. I entered the inn, hoping to get food, for by now it was two o'clock in the afternoon; but the landlady told me that she had nothing she could give me, and advised me to drive on to Maybole. However, she allowed me a glass of beer.

After drinking it I made for the grocer's shop. The grocer's son had been one of my best friends. There was a pretty girl behind the counter, and I found she was a niece of my old friend. I asked where he was and how he was, and she told me he had gone to Canada many years before. I asked after my other acquaintances, and found that one had gone to Australia, another to Simla, another to the United States. I went on asking, but every man of my own age seemed to have left the place and to have left Scotland. I enquired who was in the big house, and was told that it had been turned into a convalescent home for workmen; the sole improvement in the life of the place since I had left it. I walked along to the pretty little church at the end of the street, and returning passed the village hall, where I had learned dancing: Triumph, Petronella, the Flowers of Edinburgh, the Eightsome Reel, the Highland Schottische, Valeta, La Militaire, the Circassian Circle, all as dead now as the village itself. I thought of the crowded dances in the brightly lit ballroom, and it seemed impossible that they could ever have taken place. Perhaps there are dances there still, but as I walked through the ghost of the village, where no human being showed his face, I could scarcely believe it. During that long past winter there seemed to have been dances every week. It was not that I had been particularly happy in the place; I hated my work, and did not like most of the people, who were sly and ill-natured under a cloak of boisterousness. But boisterousness, no matter how calculating, is better than slovenly decay, and it is sad to see a community once full of acrimonious vigour slowly dying or almost dead.

I stopped at another village a little distance away, where I had often gone walking for the pleasure of looking at its pretty gardens. It, too, was neglected and forlorn. For the sake of the experiment, and with no real hope, I went into the inn and asked the landlady, a slatternly, harassed-looking woman, still young, whether she could give me anything to eat.

"Hm, hm, what wad ye want?" she asked defensively.

I suggested various things, cold beef, ham and eggs, cold ham. She shook her head and said at last:

"I could gi'e ye an e-egg."

But I needed more than an e-egg to still my hunger, and turned the car's head in the direction of Maybole.

Whether the decay of the villages of Scotland is general, I cannot say; if it is not, it is strange that the two I know best should have chosen to succumb as they have done; and statistics show that even in the last two decades the country population has been drifting to the towns, though the towns have simultaneously shown an increased percentage of unemployment. To that one must add the drainage of emigration, which in the village I have been speaking of seems to have accounted for almost every man of my generation. It is alarming to see the life of a nation insensibly and silently dying in this way. But I shall postpone considering this problem until I come to Glasgow, where decay flourishes in a genuinely impressive luxuriance.

In Maybole I ate and took the road to Ayr. I was aware of that town long before I reached it, and it was amid a huddle of dusty bungalows and villas, in a suburban street crammed with parked cars, that I stumbled on Burns's cottage. I added my car to the line, dodged the roaring traffic, and queued up for the turnstile. Behind the turnstile I found a long, low, ugly shed-like erection, where one could have tea and buy mementoes. The place was packed; in the blazing

sun hordes of people were wandering about the court-
yard behind the bars like tame animals; and the queue
lined up to sign their names in the visitors' book was
so long and so dense that one had to fight to get in
through the door of Burns's house. Large family
groups were standing in this pious line to record their
names in the book; the main expense in the keeping
up of the shrine must be stationary, I imagine. I butted
through the two little rooms along with my fellow-
worshippers and butted out again, having seen nothing
except the extreme smallness of the windows and the
darkness of the rooms, and a general effect of cleanliness, a swept and dry impression. It was so unlike my
expectation of a visit to Burns's cottage that I could
hardly believe in it, and only when I was out again
and had time to compose myself did I see that this
was exactly what the cult of Burns worship was bound
to turn into in a commercialised, newspaper-reading,
bus-driven, cinema-educated age. It is difficult to see
what makes it so ridiculous, for the whole business is
excellently organised. But one wonders how the
management will deal with this enormous traffic in
another fifty years' time, presuming that it goes on increasing. The cottage will certainly have to be enlarged, or else the price of admission raised until only
the well-to-do can get in. There seems no third alternative except demolition. The cottage itself is a neat
and tidy little structure seen from outside, the only
aspect of it that I could catch. Unlike Abbotsford, it
looks like a house in which a human being could live

with decency and dignity. In a setting of green fields it would be as charming as many a little farm-house in the remoter isles. In a suburban street it is one of the most ludicrous and pathetic sights in Scotland. Whether at some earlier stage a clear space could have been marked off and kept round this shrine, and the suburb been deflected, I do not know; but a country which pays such universal homage to its national poet could surely have managed that. The best thing would be for the whole nation reluctantly and reverently to pull the poet's birthplace down, on a day of decent mourning. But that is an impossible ideal.

The whole problem of the Burns cult in Scotland is a peculiar one, and I may as well animadvert upon it here, since no book about Scotland can avoid it. Burns was a great poet, and a character of great like-ableness and charm. He was also a man whose life and poetry are very difficult to separate; for the best of his poetry sprang directly out of his life. He expressed more perhaps than any other poet his workaday char-acter in his poetry, throwing into it his daily hopes, fears, humours, affections, lusts, repentances, despairs, sentimentalities. With such a figure to work on, it was easy for the popular imagination to substitute the man, or an idealised effigy of him, for the whole Burns, for-getting that the poet was an essential part of him and that his actual life could not have been what it was if he had not possessed genius. This is roughly what has happened. To every Scotsman Burns is a familiar figure, a sort of household god, and most Scotsmen, I suppose, could reel off a few proverbial tags of his poetry, and one or two of his songs set to music. But that is all. This public effigy, in which the lover, the boon-companion and the democrat are the main ingredients, with a hard-working farmer in the background, but all subdued to respectability by time, is the real object of worship of the Burns cult. It is not a literary cult, but a social one. It has very little to do with Burns, and is concerned chiefly with the perpetuation of a myth. In that myth Burns becomes an ordinary man like his devotees, which he was not. He also becomes a successful lover and a free and glorious companion, which everybody would like to be. His myth is thus based on a firm foundation of sanctified illusion and romantic wish fulfilment. This legendary figure is a Scotsman who took upon him all the sins of the people, not to redeem them, but to commit them as ideally as they should be committed, that is, freely and guiltlessly, in an imaginary world beyond good and evil, a Paradisal Kailyard with a harmless domesticated serpent; for even to the most respectable of Burns's worshippers, to elders and ministers of the Kirk, Burns's sins are in a special category, and his fornications have the prescriptive right of King David's. He was a scapegoat driven out to sweet pastures, while the people elected to remain in the wilderness; a god who sanctified the meagre indulgences of the many by unlimited loving and drinking.

This is not an unfair description of what Burns means to Scotland as a racial myth. The Burns of popular legend is an imaginative incarnation of a people's desires, unfulfilled in life. It has no fundamental resemblance to Burns himself. Burns was not, for the age he lived in, an immoderate drinker; nor was he a careless lover, and he perpetually cursed the weaknesses in himself which his admirers glorify. He had, like all poets of equal greatness, a keen and sure moral sense fed by a universal human sympathy such as no other Scotsman has possessed. His life was not a happy one, but filled with misery and disappointment, which he bore bravely. However, I am not concerned here with Burns, but with his legend, which is an important social phenomenon.

Now it might be held that this myth, since it fulfils a need in the life of Scotland, is probably salutary. On the other hand, it is fairly clear that the association of Burns's name with the annual junketings that take place on January 25th gives them a touch of hypocrisy. Without Burns as an excuse, they certainly could not take place; and if Burns had not been a sentimentalist as well as a great poet, they might never have taken place at all. For the sentimentalist is the groundwork of the myth which has been built up round Burns, and Burns the sentimentalist is now so necessary to it that he has become a vested interest, jealously preserved like all vested interests. This explains the extraordinary fury which greeted Mrs. Catherine Carswell's excellent life of the poet a few years ago. She trenched on a vested interest by showing Burns as a human being. From a purely literary point of view, the cult is merely an obstructive nuisance. But a blow-out every January 25th is a pleasant enough break in the monotony of a people's existence, especially if it is accompanied by a general and harmless discharge of emotion.

The myth of Burns would not have risen at all, however, if Scotsmen had not an exceptionally powerful myth-making faculty. The history of Scotland is filled with legendary figures, actual characters on which the popular imagination has worked, making them its own and by doing so transfiguring them. Wallace and Bruce, Mary Stuart and Prince Charlie are not so much historical characters as figures in an unwritten ballad: they have taken on an almost purely poetical reality, and are semi-inventions like Mary Hamilton and the Bonny Earl of Moray, the originals of whom we know to have existed historically, but who are now part of a song. Sometimes the basis on which these legends arose was paltry enough, but that did not affect the stability or the beauty of the legend. These myths never took as their foundation a moral hero: Knox, the most important figure in Scottish history, and one of the greatest, has had many lies told about him, but he has never been the theme of a poetical fiction. It is heroism, beauty and grace, generally heightened by weakness or misfortune, that the communal poetic faculty of Scotland prefers to work upon. At the beginning, when Scotland was conscious of its growing power, the theme of legend was successful heroism against odds; later, when it felt its power slipping from it, or quite vanished, its imagination turned to the spectacle of beauty in misfortune and the tragedy of a lost cause. These legends signified more than they said, like all legends, and though the theme might be Wallace and Bruce, or Mary Stuart and Prince Charlie, the mood which chose them was the mood of a nation, a nation in the first case conscious of power and in the second of weakness.

This legendary character of Scottish history distinguishes it very sharply from English history, which is concerned soberly with actual events and changes; and it must argue an unusually strong communal poetic power in the Scottish people. England has a great poetic literature, and Scotland a relatively poor one; but in the mass, if one accepts the evidence of history, the English are a prosaic race, and in the mass the Scots are strongly poetical. It is extremely difficult to give any satisfactory justification for such a statement. The average Scotsman certainly shows no more sign of poetic qualities than the average Englishman. He is even more obdurately practical, and even more ashamed of expressing his feelings except on such sanctified occasions as a Burns or a St. Andrews Night. Yet there are whole tracts of Scotland's scenery and history which are woven with legend. The existence of the ballads, and the fact that they constitute the greatest body of poetry in Scots literature, is the most concrete argument that I can advance for this theory. Scotland is a country whose past has been moulded by poetry, but which has produced very few poets. The poetry which pervades its history is purely romantic. The Industrial Revolution cut clean across that poetry, destroying it, and destroying, too, the faculty of communal myth-making which was its source. It may be that the age of poetry in Scotland is over and the age of the poet has come, or may come if Scotland as a nation does not disappear before that can happen. At least one may say that no poet in Scotland now can take as his inspiration the folk impulse that created the ballads, the people's songs, and the legends of Mary Stuart and Prince Charlie. He has no choice but to be at once more individual and less local.

From Burns's cottage to Glasgow I was accompanied almost all the way by signs of Industrialism, and being already exhausted by my efforts to do homage to Burns, I felt no temptation to stop and regard them closely. Ayr seemed to me as I passed through it a pleasant country town imprisoned among suburbs which had been lifted complete from Glasgow and set down on every side. The streets stretched on and on; it seemed that I would never come to the end of them; and only after a quarter of an hour did I realise that I was in Prestwick, a seaside resort which, when I had seen it last, about fifteen years before, enjoyed a separate existence of its own. The main road that now runs through both towns, strung with houses all the way, is a glaring concrete waste, and the soil round about it has the angry inflamed look which one often finds in raw new suburbs. This road and these houses were created to serve the pleasures of industrial man. To such places the Glasgow magnate retires for the week-end towing his favoured typist, a big balloon attended by a little balloon, to enjoy amid concrete, dust and the hoots of motor-cars the amenities of love and seclusion. The Sunday golfer comes here, and the business-like drinker, who as he sits in his hotel window can see all the world whizzing by in motor-cars and buses. One can feel in such places successive waves flowing over one from industrial Glasgow, invisible waves as real as those stationary waves of house-tops in Prestwick which rose at the command of the wealthy pleasure-seeker. Determined to commune with nature in his leisure, he had finally no choice but to create a huge town in which to do it with comfort. It is a curious reflection that in an industrial country without traditions the desire for pleasure can create towns as sordid in a different way as Motherwell or Airdrie.

After Prestwick, Kilmarnock, a grimy, tumble-down place with an air of general slatternliness, but full of character, was a great relief. I passed many houses on the main road which were undisguised slums; but—it may have been because the houses were of such an extraordinary variety of shapes and sizes, some tall, some squat, some straight, some crooked—they gave the impression of being more endurable, more comfortable than the vertical, high, gaunt tenement slums of Glasgow. Poverty which does not hide itself in closes and alleys, but walks about the street openly, as it does in Kilmarnock, is more human than the specialised poverty which is produced by large cities, where the poor live in their tenements or their streets as in compounds, and are cut off from the general life of the community by a hundred barriers of custom and psychological necessity created by their economic condition. In his account of his visit to London in 1863, the year of the Great Exhibition, Dostoievsky describes the condition of such people with a truth that, allowing for one or two differences, still applies to the slum-dwellers of Glasgow.

"The populace is everywhere the populace," he said, "but in London everything is so colossal and so glaring that you really feel something which before you had only imagined. You see something which is no longer even the populace. You can only note the loss of self-consciousness: a loss systematic, humbly borne, and encouraged. And as you look at these pariahs of society, you feel that the time is still far distant when prophecy will touch them—when they shall be given palm-branches and white raiment; and that for long they will send up their cry to the throne of the Almighty, 'How long, O Lord, how long?'. . . They themselves know this, and meanwhile take their vengeance on society as underground sectarians, Mormons, Shakers, etc. We are amazed at the stupidity shown by people in joining the Shakers and similar bodies. It does not occur to us that what we are dealing with is a separation from our recognised system of society—a separation, obstinate and unconscious, for the sake of salvation at whatever cost; an instinctive separation accompanied by horror of and aversion to us. The millions of people, abandoned and driven away from the feast prepared for men, jostling and trampling one another in the underground darkness into which they have been cast by their elder brethren, grope and knock at any door whatever, seeking a way out, so as to avoid choking in the dark cellar. This is their last despairing effort to come to their own, to separate themselves from everything, even from human likeness—provided they can live their own lives; provided they can get away from us."

"Provided they can get away from us," if by "us" one understands the present framework of society. The poor no longer knock at the strange doors that Dostoievsky mentions; they do not become Shakers and Mormons; instead they have hardened into a caste with rigid laws which are not derived from any idea, however ridiculous, but simply from the bare fact of their economic and social condition. The sole impulse behind this convention, a historical convention embracing several generations now, is that of "getting away from us." The movement which has done most in the last half-century to soften this exclusiveness of the very poor and humanise them is Socialism. The very poor are almost more hard to convert to Socialism than the very rich, it is true; partly because they are too sunk in hopelessness to open their minds to an idea, and partly because they cherish their exclusiveness as something which has become necessary to them. But Socialism, once they embrace it, does make them feel that they are a part of society, at least potentially. The most difficult thing to convince a very poor man, whose forebears have lived in a slum for generations, is that society is not a pitiless cast-iron scheme in which the position of all the classes is fixed for all time. It was this conviction, grounded on hard experience, which helped to harden the exclusiveness of the slum-dweller into a rigid convention. The slightest breach in it produces a decisive effect, and we have to thank the work of countless unknown Socialist propagandists for that. Such changes of heart do not, of course, solve the problem of poverty itself; but they bring nearer the possibility of its solution.

I have quoted this passage from Dostoievsky because it will serve as the main text of my remarks on Glasgow, which is still the most representative city in industrial, that is, modern Scotland. After leaving Kilmarnock I did not take long in reaching the outskirts of it. A stretch of bare green hilly Covenanting country still lies almost unspoilt, with its lonely farms, to the south-east of Glasgow, but it is dwindling; the petrol-stations along the roadside steadily thickened; and beside one of them I found, but did not recognise at first, a little country tea-room to which I had often walked out from Glasgow on Sundays fifteen years before, quite a long walk then. I stopped for old times' sake and ordered tea. The little house was quite changed; new rooms had been added; and it was now so obviously a place of call for motorists, not for walkers, that I was almost afraid to ask the proprietress about certain of my old acquaintances, whom I had once met there. They seldom came now, she told me: one does not walk for miles over fields and moorlands to join a crush of motorists.

In a few minutes I was in the outskirts of Glasgow. As I threaded the streets the whole town seemed to me to be much bigger than before, but at the same time emptier. I arrived at the house of an old friend in Jordanhill in time to have a second tea with him and his family in the garden. The sun was still pouring down as hotly as ever.

CHAPTER IV

GLASGOW

1

Scottish cattle are sleek and proud,
    Through flowery fields at ease they range.
The unemployed must show themselves
    Each morning at the Labour Exchange.

The Scottish pulpits are as full
    As a drove of fatted stirks.
The unemployed are empty as
    The Sunday sermons and the kirks.

Scottish adultery de luxe,
    Reported, is devoid of grace.
The unemployed cannot afford
    Marriage lines to save their face.

A Scottish bullock has a look
    About him that you will not see
In workless men shuffling their feet
    Outside some public W.C.

A Scottish bullock ends his days
    Slain by a skilled hygienic hand.
God looks after the unemployed
    When they can neither walk nor stand.

Our stirks shall yet sing Scots Wha Hae
    In kilts. Our lustier bulls and stallions
We'll educate at Balliol.
    The rest shall swell the Kirk's battalions.

Praise God from whom all blessings flow,
Praise Him all bullocks here below,
Praise Him in chief the Scottish Kirk,
For He is kind to stot and stirk.

This book is the record of a journey, and my intention in beginning it was to give my impressions of contemporary Scotland; not the romantic Scotland of the past, nor the Scotland of the tourist, but the Scotland which presents itself to one who is not looking for anything in particular, and is willing to believe what his eyes and his ears tell him. Now it is possible to maintain a fairly fresh and objective outlook if one has had no previous connection with the thing one is contemplating, and is not influenced by memories calling one's attention to this or that. But if one has lived for fifteen years in a place there is an end of objectivity, one's latest impression is merely a thin layer super-imposed on a solid mass of memory which has already hardened into a shape of its own, and that shape is the crystallised image of what one is contemplating: no new glance can change it very greatly. I lived in Glasgow for fifteen years, and the only way in which I can give any picture of it is by digging into a whole series of impressions, old and new, and one buried beneath another. The advantage of this method is that it will show Glasgow from a number of sides; the disadvantage is that I shall have to forgo objective observation; but I could not have avoided that in any case. This will make my picture of Glasgow more detailed than that of any other city I shall write about;

but that again is as it should be, for Glasgow is in every way the most important city in modern Scotland, since it is an epitome of the virtues and the vices of the industrial regions, which comprise the majority of the population. A description of Scotland which did not put Glasgow in the centre of the picture would not be a description of Scotland at all.

Yet at the same time Glasgow is not a typically Scottish town; the worst of the many evils with which it festers were not born of the soil on which it stands or of the people who live in it—a mixed population of Lowlanders, Highlanders, and Irish—but of Industrialism; and in writing about it I shall be writing about a particular area of modern civilisation which is independent of national boundaries, and can be found in England, Germany, Poland, Czecho-slovakia and most other countries as well as on the banks of the Clyde. This No Man's Land of civilisation comprises in Scotland an area which, though not very large in extent, is very densely populated. In one way it may be said that this area *is* modern Scotland, since it is the most active and vital part of Scotland as well as the most populous: the proof of its vitality being that it influences rural Scotland in all sorts of ways, while rural Scotland has no effective influence on it. But from another point of view one may say that it is not Scotland at all, or not Scotland in particular, since it is merely one of the expressions of Industrialism, and Industrialism operates by laws which do not recognise nationality. To say that is to say that Scotland is in the same position as most other European countries, except those which are still mainly agricultural. One part of its life is traditional and closely bound to the soil; another part is modern and has no immediate bond with the soil. Glasgow is consequently far more like Manchester than like Edinburgh. It is more like a manufacturing town anywhere in Europe than like a Scottish town which has preserved the old traditions of life. If the picture is sordid, then, the reader should remember this.

The spectre of Industrialism has kept on appearing in this book, and its appearance may possibly give the impression that I look upon Industrialism as completely evil, and a thing that should be speedily abolished, so that everybody might return to a more simple and healthy way of life. As I shall have a great deal more to say about Industrialism in this chapter, I should state my attitude to it as clearly as possible now. By Industrialism I mean the distinctively modern form of capitalist production and exchange which was set going over a century ago by a generally sanctioned greed such as the world had never seen before, called competition, and went on perpetuating itself in security once that greed had achieved the logical infallibility of a law. In working itself out, this process took no regard of human life, unless when it was compelled to do so; it devastated whole tracts of the country-side, and sucked the life and youth out of the rest; it huddled up as quickly and cheaply as it could great deserts of towns, quite unsuitable for human habitation; and it set its mark on several generations of the men, women and children by whose work it lived, in shrunken bodies and trivial or embittered minds. In return for this it increased vastly the total wealth of the world, and raised considerably the general standard of comfort in those countries where it prevailed. If Industrialism were suddenly to stop now, and we had to judge it by its past history, it would appear a mad dream, without justification. But a historical process incarnated in the flesh and blood of whole peoples cannot stop until it has worked itself out. Nor can it be stopped from outside by deliberate reason or good-will, and another and apparently better system substituted for it. It can at most be directed towards its natural desirable end, and the conditions for the realisation of that aim are present, it seems to an increasing number of people, in our time. Industrialism as at present managed is breaking down under the weight of the problems it has created without solving, and there is a growing belief among all classes of people that it must be consciously controlled if disaster is to be avoided, and the potential good in the system realised. The logical end of Industrialism is a state of general wealth and leisure. The American technologists have proved that that is theoretically possible, and Major Douglas, in his programme of Social Credit, has outlined a way of realising it peacefully. Socialist and Communist writers of all shades base their doctrines of social improvement on the same assumption—that is, that Industrialism, or the system of modern capitalist production, can be so used that it will benefit everybody, and turn from a curse into a blessing. Industrialism is therefore a thing which it would be an act of madness to discard in favour of a simple agricultural ideal of society, if that were possible. It is our chief earnest of the future, and the whole problem of the future centres in it. That is another reason why industrial Scotland is more important than the rest of Scotland. The main battle of the present is being fought out in it.

If, then, I paint a dark picture of Industrialism in the succeeding chapters, it is simply in the hope that the evils of present-day Industrialism may be realised and the necessity for taking it in hand brought home as vividly as possible to the reader. And if, in my description of the rural community of the Orkneys, which will come later, the colours will be pleasing, that is partly because they are actually so, but mainly because I wish to deepen the darkness of my picture of industrial Glasgow by contrasting with it a normal traditional mode of existence. The future, whatever it may be, will not be like the small-holding Belloc and Chesterton paradise of Orkney. Life there is far more harmonious and satisfying, it is true, than in any other place I found in my journey. It confirms Belloc's and Chesterton's claim that Distributism is a humanly desirable economic system. But for its realisation that system requires special conditions; these conditions are present in Orkney: they are not present in Glasgow or Dundee or Manchester. Nor is it conceivable that they will ever be.

With this explanation I can now go on to give my impressions of Glasgow, some old and some new, and mostly, I am afraid, painful.

II

I shall begin with my earliest impressions of Glasgow, for they are still the most vivid and reproduce, I imagine, the first instinctive response to Industrialism of anyone who has been brought up quite beyond reach of it. Later in life we become used to things which shocked us at first, and it is impossible for an industrial town-dweller born in an industrial town to realise the full squalor of his surroundings; he could not live in them if he did, for there is in everyone a necessity to form an attachment to the patch of earth and stone around him. Yet that necessity signifies nothing more than a fundamental human impulse which has existed ever since man settled down in one place and made a home and friends; it is no argument for the goodness of any place; even some slum-dwellers have it. As I continued to live in Glasgow I therefore acquired a liking for it, and that very much influenced my later impressions of it, making me reject, partly out of gratitude, partly out of an unconscious desire to spare my own feelings, the more unpleasant ones. I shall try, for the sake of truth, to correct that bias now.

But at the beginning, when I arrived in Glasgow

straight from Orkney, I had no self-protective apparatus for selecting my impressions, and was stunned by a succession of sights which I frantically strove not to see. The main problem which puzzled me at that time was how all these people could live in such places without feeling ashamed. The street my family lived in was in a respectable suburb on the South Side. Most of the people in it were better-paid clerks, shopkeepers, foremen, buyers, commercial travellers: a respectable church-going lot intent on making money and rising, as the saying goes, in the world. They lived in what seemed to me comfort: that is, they had several rooms in their houses, containing sofas, arm-chairs, pianos, pictures and knick-knacks of all kinds. When they went out they were well-dressed. But the streets they walked through, the sky above them, the ground beneath their feet, the house-walls on either side of them were so squalid (even in a respectable suburb) that for a long time I could not reconcile the personal neatness and cleanliness of these people with the surrounding filth, and attributed even to the most self-satisfied among them a feeling of shame which they did not possess at all (though I am convinced that it exists as a customary suppression in most respectable people who live in places like Glasgow). They gave me somewhat the same feeling as I would have if I were told that a handsome, groomed and curled, socially popular, top-hatted, frock-coated pillar of business and the Church lived in a lavatory. After I had been in Glasgow for a few years I lost this feeling, but I still think it was natural. For

one of the distinguishing marks of Industrialism is the
permanent contrast between the people who live amidst
it, if they are sensitive in any degree or even wish to
exist in decency, and all their surroundings. As these
people cease to feel the painfulness of this contrast—
and they are bound to do so—they inevitably become
insensitive; and I think one may assert without being
unfair that the middle- and upper-classes of towns like
Glasgow, where dirt and squalor are an inseparable
and normal part of one's life, even if one has a bath
where one can wash them off, or a commodious house
where one can forget them, have a sort of comfortable
insensitiveness which cannot be found in any other
class or in any other place. There may be many intelligent and humane men and women in these classes, but
somewhere or other they are blunted or dead; they have
blind-spots as big as a door: the door of their office or
of their house. They cannot help that; it is not their
fault, but the fault of a system which forces them to
gather money out of the dirt. But the self-protective
need to ignore this involves a deliberate blunting of
one whole area of their sensibility.

This applied, I found, not only to the very rich, but
to all classes of individuals in Glasgow whose main
ideal was respectability or rising in the world. In such
people the wish to get on was not merely a natural
desire, but the chief article in an exalted mystical faith,
an orthodoxy which it would have been mere vicious
perversity or worse not to subscribe to. Inherited
Calvinism was at the bottom of their contemptuous

reprobation of anyone who, out of weakness or amiability or scruple, refrained from striving to his utmost to make money; for their attitude to such people was indistinguishable from that of the elect to the damned a century before. The word "success" had accordingly the same mystical inviolability to them as the word "service" has since taken on among Rotarians: and even then the two words had established an *entente* among the young, striving men who attended such institutions as the Y.M.C.A., where business and religion had always gone hand in hand. I can still remember (I was about eighteen at the time) one of the most blatant of these young strivers pouring out his heart to me as we walked to our work one morning through Eglinton Street, a long and dreary slum. He began by asking me what I thought was the greatest thing in the world, and when I could not think of a reply, he exclaimed: "*I* think it's service!" I had no idea what service meant then, for the Rotarians had not been heard of, and we had an argument which I have forgotten; but in that fantastic conversation I can see the beginning of the process by which personal greed has been turned, in the years since, into the very quintessence of altruism. It is clear that they were already associated, and that is no doubt why success was talked of with such respect.

I have referred back this worship of success to Calvin, and I think he was largely responsible for it; but it was sanctified also by an orthodox economic theory which taught that competition was equally necessary to increase the general wealth and strengthen the individual character. These two aims, in the mind of the striver, could not be separated, but if ever his faith was challenged he was more likely to insist on its moral than its worldly advantages. For there were many people then who genuinely thought that they were seeking wealth simply in order to strengthen their character, and so every new success was a tangible proof to them that the strengthening process was going on. A rise in salary was a moral rise; a business promotion, a promotion in spiritual grace. On the other hand, if one mentioned the moral ideal of Socialism to them they would reply that economics had nothing to do with morality, and alternatively or simultaneously that Socialism was immoral, since it did not strengthen the character. The truth is that all economic or political theories, however stripped of moral assumptions, accrete a whole body of moral prejudices and emotions round them in the course of their existence. The *laissez-faire* economists could separate economics and morality with the most satisfactory neatness, but the actual people who by their labour maintained a system based on *laissez-faire* could not achieve that feat, since they were moral beings. So they had either to give *laissez-faire* a high ethical sanction, like the people of whom I have been speaking, or else regard it as evil, like the trade-unionists and Socialists whom I came to know later.

But what raised this religion of getting-on to a really intense faith was the squalor of the surroundings amid which the go-getter lived. The immediate goal that he

set before him was not great wealth, but rather respectability, and all his environment reminded him of its
opposite. In no place can respectability be a more
intense passion than in a town which at every step
one takes suggests the very things it fights against: open
filth, disorder and degradation. The pushing young
Glasgow man felt that he was directly fighting all that
this filth, disorder and degradation finally meant: that
is, the slums. He could not get away from the slums
by ordinary walking on the horizontal plane, for they
would always be there when he came back; he could
only get away from them by climbing: and in climbing above them he was scoring a symbolical victory
over them. In his climb he would have been false to
his cause if he had foregone an advantage, even
though he knew it injured somebody else; his whole
ethic would have been imperilled. That a belief like
this was bound to engender insensitiveness is so
obvious that I shall make no further apology for saying
that it has actually done so.

At the time when I came to Glasgow I could not,
of course, know all this, but I read, in the faces of
almost every man and youth I met, even in the faces
of boys of my own age (I was fourteen), this creed of
success which was quite new to me. I had come from
a country community where it was a tradition among
the small farmers to help one another when help was
needed, either with labour or their own goods, and
where the only recognised enemy was the landlord, if
he happened to be a bad one. In Glasgow, in the

particular class I was thrown among first, I found that one's neighbour was one's worst enemy, and one's employer, if not exactly one's best friend, at least the man best worth while keeping in with. In the islands it was considered contemptible to steal a march on your neighbour and tasteless to push yourself forward; but I found that here these things were thought not only permissible but a mark of virtue. I could not reconcile these traits with the kindness and courtesy (outside business) of many of the people who possessed them; and it seems to me still that they are irreconcilable. This division in the nature of these people was due directly to the corrupting influence of Industrialism.

I felt all this very clearly, far more clearly than I could feel it now, but quite blindly. I felt at the same time something else, which was much more terrifying. The best way I can put it is that these people seemed to have all passed through the slums, and to bear the knowledge of the slums within them. On their faces, which were different from the faces I had known before, I thought I could see, quite clearly displayed, a depraved and shameful knowledge, a knowledge which they could not have avoided acquiring, I can see now, but of which they were for the most part unaware. This may sound, to anyone who has lived all his life in an industrial town, exaggerated or wildly improbable; to others it will seem a truism. At any rate I felt this somewhat terrifying warning in people's faces before I had actually seen a slum, for it was several weeks after I came to Glasgow, when I found a post in an office, that I first came in contact with the slums as I walked to and from my work. After that I passed through one of the worst of them twice daily. For it is almost impossible (or was at that time) for anyone working in Glasgow to avoid passing through a slum on his way to and from work, unless he lives in the West End. The people I met did so, for they lived on the South Side, and all the main thoroughfares leading from the town to the South Side were slums or semi-slums.

This depraved knowledge which I found in people's faces was frightening mainly, I think, because the knowledge was concealed from its possessors, and was like a dangerous thing, always with them, whose existence they ignored. Later I came to know Socialists who did not conceal their knowledge of the slums, but talked of it openly, and their faces had not the look I have been trying to describe. When I became a Socialist it was as if in clearly recognising an outer danger I had killed an inner fear, and it was this, I think, which made the little Socialist gatherings I went to more light-hearted than the ones I had been accustomed to before. But at the time I am speaking of I knew nothing about Socialism, and like everybody else I stubbornly set myself not to see what was before my eyes every day. This in time produced a sense of inward squalor, the reflection of the outward misery that I pushed away from me; and finally I reached a stage where I almost ignored my surroundings, lost the natural delight in my eyes which I had once had, and shielded my senses by shutting them off from what perpetually violated them. I tell this because I feel sure the same thing happens to everybody in an industrial town. All one's surroundings there drive the senses in upon themselves and blind them to one thing after another, until they perform only a utilitarian function. This is bound to happen whether one is conscious of it or not. The great majority of industrial town-dwellers, rich and poor, are unconscious of it; and it is this that makes their response to experience so unlike that both of the artist and of the ordinary peasant, who can still look at things with more than a specialised, classifying eye.

All these things, and doubtless many others which were too subtle for my mind to catch or my memory to re-create, went to produce my first impression of the people I met in Glasgow, making me feel that they were sad and incomprehensible distortions of nature. I describe these impressions because I think that that first criticism of industrialism was immediate and clear, and is the typical response of anyone who comes straight to a town like Glasgow from the country. He feels at once that this life is barbarous and degrading, until the unanimous opinion of the people round him that it is perfectly normal works upon him, and he accepts it.

III

The refuse that one finds scattered in the streets of an industrial town has always seemed to me to tell a great deal about it, and to be in a humble way a synopsis of its life. One finds there a miscellaneous and yet representative collection which is very revealing, though it can have little resemblance to the franker contents of medieval or Renaissance streets. Scraps of newspaper, cigarette ends, rims of bowler hats, car tickets, orange peel, boot soles, chocolate paper, fish-and-chip paper, sixpences, broken bottles, pawn tickets, and various human excretions: these several things, clean and dirty, liquid and solid, make up a sort of pudding or soup which is an image of the life of an industrial town. To this soup must be added an ubiquitous dry synthetic dust, the siftings of the factories, which is capable under rain of turning into a greasy paste resembling mud, but has no other likeness to the natural mire of a country road; for that, however unpleasant underneath one's feet, breathes freshness and has a sweet smell. Sometimes this compost is thickened still more by a brown fog permeated by the same manufactured dirt, with a smell which is neither clean nor obnoxious but is simply the generalised smell of factories. In this soup it is considered a perfectly natural thing for human beings to live.

I have passed through most of the slums of Glasgow,

but I have never done so unless when forced by necessity, and I have never attempted to investigate them, and would not do so at any price. I listened once to an argument between an Englishman and a Scotsman, both Socialists, on whether England or Scotland had the worst slums, and observed that each was hurt because the other insisted that his country bore off the palm. That taught me a lesson.

Since I began to write this book everybody whom I have asked for information about Glasgow has at once got on to the subject of the slums and enjoyed himself for an hour or two, without my being able to convince him that that was not what I really wanted. I have been told of slum courts so narrow that the refuse flung into them mounted and mounted in the course of years until it blocked all the house windows up to the second-top storey; and I have been given an idea of the stench rising from this rotting, half liquid mass which I shall not reproduce here. I have been told of choked stair-head lavatories with the filth from them running down the stairs; of huge midnight migrations of rats from one block to another; and of bugs crawling down the windows of tram-cars. All these things, I have been assured, are true, and no doubt they are; but I shall not enter into a competition with the narrators of horrors of this kind, for the appetite of moderately well-off and quite well-off people for these infamous morsels is one which has no connection with the sentiment of pity, but is likely to check rather than induce it, creating disgust in its stead. Disgust is the coldest of human emotions, colder than hatred because more self-centred. If one hates the slums one may do something about them; but if one is filled with disgust of them there is nothing but to turn away.

Moreover, it is difficult to define a slum, and a more important fact is that the majority of the population of Glasgow live in some form of poverty caused by the working of the economic system. The insanitary slums are more picturesque, and more thrillingly horrible things can be related of them; but if one could conceive the total volume of colourless or bug-coloured poverty that exists in Glasgow, as in all other cities of its kind, one would be crushed by the knowledge. We manage to live with some comfort simply because we cannot conceive it. The life of the slums is infamous, but it is freer and more various than the life of the decent poor. A slum is a poor quarter in which the people no longer take the trouble to keep up appearances. Nothing in such places makes any attempt to keep up appearances. The houses have a rotten look, and send out a complicated bouquet of mingled stenches. All that respectable society conceals is openly displayed. Language has a flat and commonplace obscenity; knowledge, however vile, is frankly expressed; passions and hatreds let themselves go. All this happens within a sort of invisible cage, whose bars are as strong as iron. It is a life which through the course of generations has acquired a settled convention; for children grow up in these places and are trained from their earliest years in the way of life which is suitable for them. The deepest hope of the decent poor is to bring up their children in a way that will give them the opportunity of a better life than their parents. What distinguishes the slum-dwellers from the decent poor is that they have quite given up this hope, that they are quite static. They see no prospect for themselves or their descendants but the slums. This is because they are the final product of a system; there is nothing beyond them; and their existence has therefore a logic with which there is no arguing.

Yet this does not mean that these people are a special class outside the bounds of humanity, but merely that they are ordinary men and women in a hopeless position, who have been placed there by the operation of a process over which they have no control. That being so, it would surely be inhuman to grudge them what enjoyment they can get, whether in drink, love, or fighting, and stupid to complain, as the benevolent sometimes do, that the hearts of these people are not at once softened by a smile or a few kind words. A natural impulse is to snatch every child away from such places; but even if that could be done the slums would fill up again; the system under which we live forces people into them with a continuous mechanical pressure, and once they are there they may give up all hope: they will become like their neighbours. The sufferings of an ordinary healthy child brought up in the slums are dreadful beyond imagination. The terror and corrupt knowledge of these children can be heard in their voices, the most desolate and discordant sound in creation. This terror breaks out in early youth, that is as soon as these boys are strong enough to fight for themselves, in revengeful violence and cruelty. This process coincides with puberty, it is automatic, and kind words and boys' clubs will never have more than a passing effect on it.

The openness of all this slum life in Glasgow makes it impossible for the respectable who come in contact with it every day not to build up some attitude to it. The general attitude is simple reprobation, an explicit declaration that all slum-dwellers are incurably depraved and outside the human pale. This attitude makes people ignore the slums as irrelevant to ordinary life, and leads to that suppression of knowledge which I read in so many faces when I first came to Glasgow. The more humane generally hold that a great deal can be done by kindness and goodwill. There are others again, also humane, who take an objective interest in the slum-dwellers as a curious species of humanity with a flavour of their own. I can give an instance of this.

When I was eighteen I stayed in the same lodgings as a young Highlander, six or seven years older than myself. With his Highland courtesy he contrived to give me very good advice and unobtrusively keep his eye on me, showing a most delicate nicety of consideration in everything which concerned us both. I was in the first stages of my conversion to Socialism and he was troubled about my state, for he was a pious

conservative. We were arguing one day about
Socialism, when he told me a story he had heard which
indirectly supported his view that things should be
left as they were. It was about a newsboy. For several
years he had stood at a certain street corner in Glasgow,
barefoot both in summer and winter. A regular
customer of his, a kind-hearted man, taking pity on
his feet blue with cold, presented him with boots and
stockings. The boy thankfully accepted them, but a
few days after he began to wear them he went down
with pneumonia and died in hospital. Now my friend,
who was one of the kindest-hearted men I have ever
known, simply regarded this as an interesting example
of low life; he was sincerely sorry for the boy, but it
never occurred to him that the boy's existence was
other than it should be, and the moral of his story
was that the *status quo* should not be interfered with.
I tell this incident because it illustrates a respectable
attitude to the slums, which though infinitely prefer-
able to the ordinary attitude of suppression, is as
strictly conditioned.

The most revolting and illuminating attitude to the
slums that I ever encountered in Glasgow was held by
a kind-hearted theosophist. Theosophists are people
who have very little difficulty in believing things, and
his belief was that the people in the slums were suffering for sins which they had committed in a former
existence, so that any betterment of their lot would
nullify this act of expiation and be spiritually wrong.
The fact that as slum-dwellers they had no knowledge

of those former sins did not matter to him in the least. Now there had been a peculiarly horrible murder committed about that time. A young woman had been found in a wood with various knife wounds on her body and the marks of a man's teeth on her throat; and it seemed to me that if some morning a police constable were to call at my innocent theosophist's house, seize him, pry open his mouth, announce: "The marks were made by your teeth," haul him off to prison and have him tried and condemned, he would be in exactly the same position as the slum-dwellers he thought of as suffering for former sins of which they could never know. The slum-dwellers are not condemned to death, it is true, but merely to lifelong imprisonment; but that is an infinitely more dreadful punishment. The more I thought of the theosophist's idea, the more I was impressed by its truth as a picture of the life of a slum-dweller. Any theory at all, however ludicrous, which attempts to account for a thing, makes us see it more completely than before. And taking away the comforting theosophical moral, it is as if an invisible police inspector had seized all the inhabitants of the slums at some stage in their lives, in infancy before they could speak, in manhood, in old age, and haled them to a judge to be sentenced for life for a crime of which they were quite unaware. They commit other crimes in plenty, no doubt, but they never committed this one, which they could not understand even if it were explained to them. That is a measure of their hopelessness.

The squalor of the slum-dwellers' lives in Glasgow is one reason for the respectable attitudes which I have tried to describe. A stronger reason is their open publication of their degradation, which springs partly from their hopelessness and partly from a feeling that it is wrong that misery and vice such as theirs should be ignored. This public flaunting of degradation is one of the things which distinguish the Scottish from the English slums. Probably it arises from a last-ditch sentiment of justice. To publish one's degradation is a moral protest. The London slums are dreary; but the Glasgow slums always hold a sense of possible menace; they take their revenge on the respectable and the rich if in nothing else in compelling them to grow a still thicker hide of insensibility and suppression. That revenge may appear small, but its effects are beyond computation. There can be hardly any decent Glaswegian but has seen some sight in passing through the slums which he afterwards wanted to erase from his memory. Such memories should be kept open, not hidden away in places where they fester, for that is the only hope both for those who suppress them and for the eventual health of society. But it is easier to say this than to do it. For the life of an average member of the respectable classes in Glasgow is a direct fight against the slums, and in that fight suppression and insensibility are invaluable weapons, and as long as society continues to be competitive they will be used. Thus the existence of the slums and of poverty in general poisons the life of a community in all sorts of hidden ways. It is this settled almost comfortable poisoned state which I have tried to give some idea of. It is the generic state of Industrialism.

IV

The slums not only penetrate the lives of all classes in Glasgow, affecting their ideas and their most personal emotions, perhaps going with them into their bedrooms, but also send out a dirty wash into the neatest and remotest suburbs and even the surrounding countryside, so that it is possible for one to feel that the whole soil for miles around is polluted. This is partly, no doubt, because the slums of Glasgow are distributed over a very large area and in a very irregular form, so that it is difficult even in the West End to get very far away from them. Some of them are on the outskirts, like Polmadie and Springburn; others occupy a large area of the centre of the town at either end of Argyle Street; the older part of the South Side is honeycombed with them from east to west; and there is another large area from the Cowcaddens to Garscube Road extending for a considerable distance into the north-west, which is the rich and fashionable quarter.

To the south-east between Polmadie and Rutherglen the city ended when I came to it first in country which could only be called slum country. (That has since been covered, much to its improvement, by new houses.) There, if one wanted to get country air, one had to walk past several squalid rows of miners' hovels among which a farmhouse had been forlornly stranded, with a piggery of surpassing stench. After that came a country road called the Hundred Acre Dyke, dotted with a few ringwormed trees, and affording a bleak prospect of smoking pits and blackened fields. This was a great resort of lovers on Sunday evenings. If one turned to the right until one passed the little town of Cathcart, now a part of Glasgow, one reached a pleasant enough country road. But the first stretch was, like the immediate surroundings of almost all industrial towns, a debased landscape in which every growing thing seemed to be poisoned and stunted, a landscape which involuntarily roused evil thoughts and seemed made to be the scene of murders and rapes.

There was another stretch of country to the northwest beyond Anniesland, which, although it was without coal-pits or factories, had for some reason the same character. There was a meanly wicked-looking wood there where lovers wandered in the evenings, and this wood was periodically infested by hooligans who spied on these young couples and sometimes tried to blackmail them. The country between Polmadie and Rutherglen was one of the most desolate of these tracts. There were several small coal-pits there, and walking on a Sunday afternoon through the black slag paths one would see stunted naked boys bathing in the filthy pools, from which rose a smell of various acids

and urine. Respectable people also took their constitutional there and stared at the tattered trees which
rose from that scabbed landscape. If one walked out
for a few miles one could get away from this scene and
into real country. But such places seemed to have an
attraction, and the crowds there were far thicker than
they were a few miles out.

The slums in a Scottish industrial town are generally to be found either near the factories or in the
oldest and most dilapidated of the tenements. Glasgow
has slums of both kinds. There are certain factories
which produce such a stench that to live near them
involves a loss of self-respect, and the surrounding
houses in such cases turn into slums. Many such
factories are scattered over the South Side. On the
other hand the tenements near the shipyards have
mostly a clean and orderly look; and one can still feel
(though they have degenerated a great deal since shipbuilding virtually stopped) that the people who lived
in them led for many years a self-respecting existence
and had a tradition. And immediately behind some
of the shipyards one may come upon green fields dotted
with trees. Shipbuilding does not pollute the air or
ravage the soil as coal-mining does, and the comparative cleanliness of his work gives the shipyard worker,
I think, a peculiar self-respect, or did at one time,
when there was something for him to do.

This extraordinarily wide distribution of the slum
areas in Glasgow may actually be good in some ways
for the spiritual health of its people. The strength

of the Socialist Party in Glasgow is probably due in part to this impossibility of getting away from the slums.

In Henry Grey Graham's *Social Life in Scotland in the Eighteenth Century,* one of the best books ever written on Scotland, there is a very attractive description of Glasgow as it was about 1730. Graham was a man who did not sentimentalise the past; indeed his picture of life in eighteenth-century Scotland is a very dark one. He quotes the testimony of Edward Burt, an "English engineer officer," who visited the city in 1726. "It has," said Burt, "a spacious carrefour where stands the cross, and going round it you have by turns the views of the four streets that in regular angles proceed from thence. The houses are faced with ashlar stone; they are well sashed, all of one model, and piazzas rise round them on either side, which gives a good air to the buildings. There are some handsome streets; but the extreme parts of the town are mean and disagreeable to the eye." He thought the town "the most uniform and prettiest" that he had ever seen. Another witness quoted by Graham—M'Ure, the first historian of Glasgow—describes the town as "sur rounded with cornfields, kitchen and flower gardens, and beautiful orchards, abounding with fruits of all sorts, which, by reason of the open and large streets, send forth a pleasant, odoriferous smell." Graham adds, with his usual common-sense realism: "Beside the substantial houses of the well-to-do citizens, with quaint picturesque Flemish architecture and crow-stepped gables, however, stood mean, dirty, and broken-down hovels to mar the beauty of the town; while in the streets stood middens, against which magistrates vainly objected, and in the gutters remained garbage seriously to spoil the 'odoriferous smell' of the fruit- and flower-scented air."

It was the Union with England that first started Glasgow on its road to prosperity. Before that Scotland had not been allowed to trade with Virginia (which was a strict English preserve). Through the trade in tobacco Glasgow increased greatly both in wealth and population. The tobacco trade collapsed in 1776 with the outbreak of the American war, plunging many of the tobacco lords into bankruptcy. But in 1754 James Watt had come to Glasgow from Greenock, and it was while he was walking in the Glasgow Green one Sunday afternoon that "the idea of the steam condenser flashed upon his mind." That Sunday walk, along with the presence of coal and iron within easy reach and the Clyde at its gate, did more than anything else to decide the subsequent fate of the town and make possible its enormous wealth and its enormous squalor. In the nineteenth century the town increased by leaps and bounds and quite haphazardly, and it is still increasing, though prosperity has left it. Before 1707 the town's population was a little over 12,500; by 1800 it was almost 80,000; now it is over a million. This rapid and enormous increase was due mainly to the neighbouring iron and coal mines, and to shipping and shipbuilding. Scottish iron is almost at a standstill; coal is declining; and shipping and shipbuilding in Britain generally have sunk so definitely that not even optimists expect them to be again what they once were, except in the event of another war. The probable consequence seems to be that Glasgow, after its rapid expansion, is fated to shrink again. A competitive system can provide for expansion; indeed expansion is a necessary condition for its smooth working. But it can make no provision at all for contraction; and if Glasgow is to decrease in size, which seems unavoidable, if Scotland, after its feverish burst of industrialism, is to relapse into a predominantly agricultural state again, which seems possible, something besides the mere operation of the competitive system will be needed to effect that transition. It is a feeling of the imminence of this problem which, among other things, has led to the spread of Nationalism. But Nationalism without a social programme, and a radical one, will be quite impotent to deal with it.

If all this were actually to happen, if industrial Scotland, having exhausted itself, were to disappear, leaving the black coal and iron country to be reclaimed by the peasant, it might seem that the immense effort of growth which we call Industrialism had been wasted: a mere brute fact of history, a devastation without meaning. But one has only to turn to Graham's picture of life in eighteenth-century Scotland to see that that is not so, and to recognise the necessity of the industrial phase. In his chapter on

"The Land and the People" he tells of the famine years which began the eighteenth century. "From one end of the country to the other the poorer classes of the population of above a million were in misery, hunger, and in the shadow of death. . . . The sheep and oxen died in thousands, the prices of everything among a peasantry that had nothing went up to famine pitch, and a large proportion of the population in rural districts was destroyed by disease and want. During these 'hungry years,' as starvation stared the people in the face, the instincts of self-preservation overpowered all other feelings, and even natural affection became extinct in crowds of men and women forced to prowl and fight for their food like beasts. People in the north sold their children to slavery in the plantations for victuals: men struggled with their sisters for a morsel of bread; many were so weak and dispirited that they had neither heart nor strength to bury their dead. On the roads were to be seen dead bodies with a morsel of raw flesh in their mouths, and dying mothers lying with starved infants which had sucked dry breasts; while numbers, dreading lest their bodies should be exposed to the birds, crawled, when they felt the approach of death, to the kirkyard, that they might have some better chance of being buried when death overtook them. . . . Even in the streets of towns starving men fell down and died." And he quotes a contemporary witness, Patrick Walker, the old Covenanter. "Through the long continuation of these manifold judgments," says Walker, "deaths and

burials were so common that the living wearied of
burying the dead. I have seen corpses drawn on sleds,
many neither having coffins or winding-sheets. I was
one of four who carried the corpse of a young woman
a mile of way, and when we came to the grave an
honest man came and said, 'You must go and help me
to bury my son; he is lien dead these two days; otherwise I will be obliged to bury him in my own yard.'
We went, and there were eight of us had two miles
to carry the corpse of this young man, many neighbours looking on, but none to help. I was credibly
informed that in the north two sisters on a Monday's
morning were found carrying the corpse of their
brother with bearing ropes, none offering to help. I
have seen some walking about till the sun-setting, and
to-morrow about six o'clock in the summer's morning
found dead, their heads lying in their hands, and mice
and rats having eaten a great part of their hands and
arms."

This is what happened in years of famine, when the
crops failed; but years of famine seem to have been
pretty frequent. In good years the ordinary people
lived in poverty far surpassing that of a modern slum.
Graham says: "In 1702 Morer, the English chaplain,
described the houses of the vulgar as 'low and feeble,
their walls made of a few stones jumbled together without mortar to cement 'em, so ordered that it does not
cost much more time to erect such a cottage than to
pull it down,' without chimneys, and only holes in the
turf-covered roofs for smoke to pass. His description

will apply to the houses of the people through a great part of the eighteenth century. The hovels of one room were built of stones and turf, without mortar, the holes in the wall stuffed with straw, or heather, or moss, to keep out the blasts. The fire, usually in the middle of the house floor, in despair of finding an exit by the smoke-clothed roof, filled the room with malodorous clouds. The cattle at night were tethered at one end of the room, while the family lay at the other on heather on the floor. The light came from an opening at either gable, which, whenever the wind blew in, was stuffed with brackens or an old bonnet to keep out the sleet and blast. The roofs were so low in northern districts that the inmates could not stand upright, but sat on the stones or three-legged stools that served for chairs, and the huts were entered by doors so low and narrow that to gain an entrance one required almost to creep. Their thatching was of ferns and heather, for the straw was all needed for the cattle. Yet, foul, drab, and fetid as they were, the people liked these hovels for their warmth." This dirt and poverty gave rise to a great deal of disease; and the people, being religious, accepted the epidemics that swept large numbers of them away as visitations from God. Women grew old and lost their looks very early. And the whole country got a bad name for the skin disease that infested it.

Graham ascribes a great part of this poverty to ignorance and superstition. "Piety did not uproot this inveterate sluggishness of farmer and labourer; it seemed rather to dignify dirt and consecrate laziness.

The people believed that disease was due to the hand of God, instead of being due to the want of using their own hands. They held that every season of dearth was owing to Providence rather than to their own improvidence. They protested that weeds were a consequence of Adam's fall, and that to remove docks, wild mustard, and nettles was to undo the divine curse. They threshed the corn with the flail, and winnowed it by throwing it up in the air, rather than use the outlandish fanners which Meikle had set up in 1770; because 'it was making Devil's wind,' contravened Scripture, which said, 'The wind bloweth where it listeth,' and took the 'power out o' the hands o' the Almighty.'"

To read of such past poverty and wretchedness shows what an immense advance has been made since by the increase of things like knowledge and education (which there is a disposition to depreciate at present) and by Industrialism itself, in spite of its evils; and it also gives a reasonable hope that the improvement will continue, a hope all the more justified because we are now in a position to see more clearly perhaps in what direction it lies. The unemployed engineer on the Clyde to-day is better off than the employed peasant in the early eighteenth century; and that is due partly to Industrialism, which has made a higher standard possible, and partly to the growth during the last two centuries of what is called the social conscience, which insists that a higher standard should actually be maintained. Left to itself the Industrial System would clearly have produced during the last decade misery on a scale that would have left Graham's picture far behind. Yet there is no doubt that the evolution of Industrialism itself, by increasing wealth generally, has helped to change our attitude to the poor and make the thought unpleasant that they should die of starvation. In a country where poverty is the norm, as it was in Scotland in the beginning of the eighteenth century, people cannot be expected to pay very scrupulous attention to the degrees of poverty, especially if destitution should be ordained and sometimes directly produced by the hand of God. Starvation in a state of potential plenty is a very different thing: a community which permitted it now would be guilty of a criminal coldness of heart. Scotland in the early eighteenth century was guilty merely of ignorance, superstition and misfortune. There was probably a narrower gulf between the rich man and the starving man then than there is to-day between the wealthy magnate and the unemployed engineer drawing his 15/3. So it seems that the social conscience, undeniable as its virtues are, operates only within narrow limits, and is content if it can be assured that people are not actually dying of starvation.

The obvious truth is that the problem at the present stage is not starvation at all. It cannot be in a world where wheat is burned and herring thrown back into the sea. Every age has its own problems, and can deal only with them. Scotland got over its starving eighteenth-century phase by applying reason to its

agriculture in the first place, and by the rise of the
Industrial System in the second. The problem of our
time is how to make the Industrial System work to
everybody's benefit. 15/3 a week can certainly keep a
single man alive; it cannot possibly provide him with
a life that is desirable. The unemployed married man
is still worse off, and his children, if they get only what
the Government allows them, are worst off of all. 8/-
is supposed to keep an unemployed man's wife, and 2/-
each believed to provide for his children, no matter
what their ages may be.

As unemployment makes up such a large part of the
present life of Scotland there can be no ignoring it in
a book such as this. One has to make some attempt to
understand what it means. About two years ago a com-
mittee appointed by the British Medical Association
laid down what it regarded as the absolute minimum
cost of food necessary for the health of a human being.
It made the discovery that a child could live healthily
on 2/8 a week, and a full-grown man on 5/11. This
would not provide a man with clothes to cover him or
a roof to shelter him, but if he had such accessories
he could live on 5/11 a week and his children on 2/8
each.

Now in a talk over the wireless in January, 1934,
Dr. Somerville Hastings reckoned that, on the figure
which the British Medical Association regarded as the
minimum "for a family of five—father, mother and
three children aged, say, six, ten, and fourteen—the
minimum cost of essential needs would be 36/4,"

while the most that his family could receive as Unemployment Insurance benefit was 29/3. The natural conclusion that he came to was that "there can be no doubt whatever that many families are really starving. I do not suggest that many, or indeed any, are short of bread, but I am certain that thousands are lacking foods that are essential for healthy growth and development. . . . A special medical examination of children in the L.C.C. elementary schools took place recently, and great satisfaction was expressed that only 6.5 per cent were considered by the doctor who examined them to be poorly nourished. We must remember, however, that the signs of under-nourishment in children take time to develop and are not always easily recognised, though they invariably leave a scar on the constitution which lasts throughout life. You will not be surprised, therefore, to learn that among elder children—that is those from the secondary schools—7.2 per cent of the boys and 12.2 per cent of the girls were reported as under-nourished."

One does not like such ways of arguing, even when they are used on the right side; and there was something repulsive in the acrimonious controversy which raged in the newspapers between the friends and the critics of the unemployed after the publication of the report I have mentioned. There one found eminent medical authorities furiously contending over a penny more or less in the menu of the poor, and accepting as the rock basis of their controversy that the poor must in no circumstances live on anything but the bare minimum: though at the same time food was being destroyed. The reply to that is:

> O, reason not the need: our meanest beggars
> Are in the poorest things superfluous:
> Allow not nature more than nature needs,
> Man's life's as cheap as beast's . . . But for true need,
> You heavens, give me patience, patience I need!

To compel people to live in starvation can be argued to be more cruel than to let them die of starvation as their ancestors did in the eighteenth century: the volume of suffering it produces is probably more. It is certain that any intelligent man at that time would have been hard put to it to lay down *on what a human being could live,* and would probably have considered it presumptuous to do so: but this problem provides no difficulty to a medical commission now, except after the publication of its report. But once the report is available—and this is the real evil—all thought of the human beings it concerns vanishes: they become mere digestive systems from which acrobatic feats more or less strenuous are required; and the only question that remains is to what extremes these digestive systems can be pushed without collapsing in despair. But the argument does not stop even there; all these digestive systems, each with human idiosyncrasies of its own—such as an insatiable yearning for steak and kidney pie—are next reduced to an impersonal and colourless but extraordinarily ascetic digestive system, and that is set up as the standard to which all of them, no matter how naturally lusty or fastidious, must conform. A myth, which one might call the digestive man, is the result. The task of health statistics is to see that this entity should never take a mouthful more than is required by his hungry and deceitful stomach. And if an unemployed man has a small family, then according to Dr. Somerville Hastings the dole is not sufficient to allow him even that minimum of a minimum.

In short, the evil of all figures dealing with human beings is that they make us forget everything but the figures. The doctor who examined the children in the L.C.C. elementary schools found *only* 6.5 per cent of them poorly nourished. In the secondary schools 7.2 of the boys and 12.2 of the girls were found to be under-nourished. What the percentage is in Glasgow I do not know, but as unemployment is far more general there than in London one may assume that it is higher. The statistician sees these percentages as figures, and "comparatively" low figures. But if one throws off the glamour of arithmetic it is easy enough to perceive in these figures thousands of boys and girls who are hungry and in bad health, and behind them fathers and mothers who cannot like very much to sit and watch their children going without necessary food which they themselves would do anything to earn by hard work, if somebody would only let them. The situation of an unemployed man and of everybody dependent upon him is one of complete helplessness.

There was a time when if a man looked round him he could get work of some kind; but now for tens of thousands there is nothing but 15/3, 23/3, 27/3, 29/3, or whatever the figure may be, and nothing they can do can alter these cast-iron hieroglyphics, which are a sort of black charm keeping them in a state of semi-animation and making them a race of "the dead on leave," "die Toten auf Urlaub," to use Rosa Luxemburg's phrase. Most of these unemployed men in Glasgow are as honest and decent, and when they have money of their own, as generous as one has any right to expect them to be. They are excellent workmen whom society has deprived of work, good fathers whom society will not allow to provide for their families, cheerful companions who live in a world where they cannot afford even the little harmless amenities which make companionship twice warmer. Their life now is a long and dreary Sunday; their hands have grown useless; their skill has dropped from them; their days have turned into an unending, inconclusive dream. The effect of one, or two, or five, or ten years of waiting for work can be seen in their attitudes as they stand at the street corners; the very air seems empty round them, as if it had been drained of some essential property; they scarcely talk, and what they say seems hardly to break the silence: the strongest impression I received of Glasgow was one of silence. In the centre of the city people are still busy, or seem to be so; but when one goes down the Clyde, to what used to be the busy shipbuilding quarter, there is hardly anything but this silence, which one would take to be the silence of a dead town if it were not for the numberless empty-looking groups of unemployed men standing about the pavements. I noticed that even the children seemed to make less noise than they used to do, as if silence had seized upon them too: or it may have been simply that they were insufficiently fed.

It was a very hot bright day when I went down to see the shipyards that once in my life I had passed every morning. The weather had been good for several weeks, and all the men I saw were tanned and brown as if they had just come back from their summer holidays. They were standing in the usual groups, or walking by twos and threes, slowly, for one felt as one looked at them that the world had not a single message to send them on, and that for them to hasten their steps would have meant a sort of madness. Perhaps at some time the mirage of work glimmered at the extreme horizon of their minds; but one could see by looking at them that they were no longer deceived by such false pictures.

I was on my way to a shipbuilding office where I had once worked for several years. During my time there had been twelve clerks in it; they had now shrunk to six, and the six were on half-time and half-pay. Like the unemployed they were all sunburnt, since they spent half of their days in enforced leisure. The office had always been a pleasant one to work in; for the cashier, an old gentleman now dead, had for fifty years or so resisted the importunities of travellers for newfangled devices such as adding-machines and filing systems, and had stuck to the methods he had found in operation when he entered the office as a junior clerk. When that could have been I have no idea, probably about 1860. We were all proud of him, and grateful for the way in which he left us to ourselves: I have never been in a little community where such an idyllic and quietistic atmosphere reigned. Something of it still remained when I paid my visit. So my old friends, instead of being embittered by the bad turn of shipbuilding, were philosophic and resigned. Nevertheless, it was sad to revisit the place and remember the time when it had been filled with hope: a hope which in it, as in a hundred other workshops and offices in the Clyde, is now hardly more than a memory. Thousands of young men started out a little over twenty years ago with the ambition of making a modest position in the world, of marrying a wife and founding a family. And thousands of them have seen that hope vanish, probably never to return for the rest of their lives. This is surely one of the most astonishing signs of our time: the disappearance in whole areas of society of a hope so general at one time that not to have it would have seemed unnatural. As for the generation of unemployed who have arisen since the war, many of them are not even acquainted with this hope.

There recently appeared a very interesting review in *Life and Letters* of a book on Spenser's *Faerie Queene*, which touched indirectly on this point. Writing about a different class, the critic said: "It seems that people are more generally interested now in the internal form of their life than in the external—careers, public service, bringing up families, supporting with dignity a recognised position in a community. There must be a great many reasons: the most obvious is the breakdown of employment, and of the social structure of life altogether. It is quite strange now to meet a young man who is straightforwardly ambitious, who thinks of his occupation as a career, and a career as his life's business." After a visit to Glasgow these words have a somewhat ironical sound: but if one could intensify a hundredfold the state described in them it would apply to the workers on the Clyde. The reviewer continues, turning from the present-day world to that of the *Faerie Queene*: "In the same way, Spenser's knights, though we could say that they had careers of a kind, and though they live in a world full of distractions, are occupied with a wholly personal and internal quest—anyone who had never heard the word 'allegory' would easily recognise that. Whatever they are doing, it is never anything settled or sensible. They live in a curious freedom. . . ." The author makes this comparison because he fancies that Spenser is a poet who should appeal particularly to the present generation, which again has an ironical sound, if one imagines Spenser being read on the Clyde. Yet, "whatever they are doing it is never anything settled or sensible" is true enough of the unemployed. "They live in a curious freedom" is true also, though it is the purely negative freedom of not having to do anything, not that of being able to do quite impossible things like the heroes of Spenser's poem. Spenser's world is impossible in one way, and the world of unemployment in another, but they have somewhere an underlying resemblance. The reviewer goes on to speak of "the shapeless landscape" of Spenser's world, "which it is unthinkable should ever be mapped"; and again one can feel the likeness to the everlasting Sunday land of the unemployed, which is like an amorphous floating island anchored to no solid ground outside it. But marooned on that island, what "personal and internal quest" can the unemployed man pursue? The meaninglessness of life there makes everything meaningless: for what sense would there be in the existence of a vast shipload of people dumped on a desert island which some obscure decree absolutely forbade them to cultivate: a floating garden of Eden in which there was nothing but forbidden trees? If they had books they might study poetry or philosophy, or try to discover, on what evidence they could gather together, the cause of their shipwreck and the reason why they were mysteriously doomed to do nothing to serve their own or the general advantage. But that is all they could do.

Once on a summer afternoon, as I watched the young men wandering among the ranges of slag-heaps outside Airdrie, I was foolish enough to wonder how it was that no sage or Mahatma had ever risen among them, for they seemed to me to have nothing to do but think. It was a fantastic speculation. A people in grinding bondage certainly try to escape from it, as the Jews did in the Old Testament. But the technique for accomplishing that feat is far more difficult now than it was in Moses' time: indeed, it is impracticable, for the unemployed, even though they number more than two millions, cannot do it by themselves: it must be done for them. But in that case, no purpose could be served by their thinking, for even thought postulates some hope. All these considerations, whether they are consciously aware of it or not, colour their mood and make it hopeless. In them the desire of the poor which Dostoievsky noted to cut themselves off from society has been finally accomplished; not by them, but by society itself. At forty, at thirty, at twenty, sometimes at birth, they are pensioned off from civilisation, and their lives consigned to inactivity and ennui.

This brings me back to the *Faerie Queene* for the last time, for in spite of the sense of delight which fills that poem, it has a deep undertone of ennui, a disease that Spenser suffered from, as we know. It may seem curious to use the *Faerie Queene* as a commentary on unemployment, but I am trying to imagine what unemployment means as a mode of life, and for the understanding of profound states of mind we have to go to poetry. One of the most eloquent cantos in the *Faerie Queene* is the one where the Red Cross Knight meets Despair in his cave, and there is line after line in the speech of Despair which, though they prefigure something else, might stand as a symbol of the life of the unemployed.

"Then doe no further goe, no further stray,
But here ly downe, and to thy rest betake . . .
For what hath life that may it loved make,
And gives not rather cause it to forsake?"

I could quote at length from this marvellous speech of Despair if it were not wanton to apply a general comment on human life to a particular class which has more misfortune to bear than it can put up with. The enforced inactivity, the loss of manual skill, the perpetual scrimping to keep alive, the slow eating away of dignity and independence, the compulsory spectacle of semi-starvation round one, in the faces of the children one has brought into the world: these are great hardships, and so urgent that they must occupy constantly the thoughts of an unemployed man; but it seems to me that the emptiness and meaninglessness of his life, to which there seems no term, must be a far deeper misery, colouring all the others. There can be no sense of reality in such a life, nothing that one can hold on to but the coming and going of the days.

v

Here I think I had better go back and give some impressions of these people, now unemployed, as I knew them years ago when they were working and Industrialism on the Clyde still seemed to have a long and vigorous life before it. I have already said all that I want to say about the business mystics whom I chanced to meet first of all; I suppose they might be described as middle-class people striving to become upper middle-class. All of them really belonged to the working class, but because their eyes were fixed on a brighter goal and they wore smartly cut suits and bowler hats instead of dungarees and caps, this fact was magically concealed from them, and if taxed with it they indignantly denied it.

Being a poorly paid clerk, I also belonged to this class, and I only came in contact with that part of the working class which acknowledges that it is working class when I joined in turn a Socialist club called the Clarion Scouts, the I.L.P., and my union, the National Union of Clerks.

If I were to try to define the difference between the class I left and the class I entered then, I should find it very difficult: but I think it would be true to say that the genuine workman had far more freedom of mind, more generosity of feeling, and a considerably more delicate sense of honour than the sham one. To unite with one's fellow-workers for a common aim, in a union or some other body, is no doubt an aim which is finally based on interest; but it is also one which demands a certain disinterestedness from the units composing it. A trade union seeks to advance the good of all its members, Socialism to secure the good of everybody, and such an ideal is by any standards higher than the ideal of mere individual self-advancement which was held by the class I had known first. That class, or such members of it as thought about the matter at all, held that in doing the best for himself a man was serving the highest interests of society; and they never saw that this was a belief so fatally convenient that it allowed a man to follow his bent as much as he pleased, while imposing upon him no obligations whatever except the obligation of keeping the law, and if he was a religious man of observing such religious commands as squared with his economic interest. His obligations, in other words, were vague and general. They were matters of belief: he believed, for instance, that God existed, that Christ died for him (if he was an evangelical Christian), that theft, murder, adultery, and various other things, such as drinking and swearing, were bad, and that the British Empire was the greatest of all institutions. He might believe also, if he liked, that Roman Catholicism was the Scarlet Woman, that mixed bathing was an abomination and Sabbath-breaking blasphemous; but as he had no urgent temptation to indulge in any of these sins except, perhaps, adultery, the avoidance of them imposed no real sacrifice on him: they were pictured and framed sins which he hung up in his life because they were an expected part of its furniture. He professed a Christianity which had no connection even with the means by which he contrived the feat of living, that is his daily business; a concern for the good of society which permitted him to do the same things that an inveterate enemy of it might have done with equal reason; and a patriotism, for the Empire or for Scotland or for both, which was merely a pleasant and warmth-giving emotion. In other words, he professed a great number of moral sentiments, but the most important part of his life, the part he spent at work, was quite uninfluenced by moral considerations, being ruled merely by considerations of legality. As most of the men I am speaking of were professing Christians, one cannot help thinking that the Scottish Church, by its weak or politic or merely worldly policy of trimming, has been largely responsible for this false state of things. There are many among the younger Scottish ministers now of whom nobody could say this; but the damage was done before their time, and I doubt whether they will be able to undo it.

Now among the trade union workers whom I met there did not exist this accepted and complacent division between profession and practice; and their relation to one another was not merely a self-seeking relation cloaked in moral sentiments, but a real moral relation. Their obligations to one another were obligations for which if necessary they had to make sacrifices. They were pledged neither to take any advantage of their neighbours, nor to rise in the world at their expense. These are moral principles, and, socially speaking, among the most fundamental of moral principles. The remarkable thing is that these trade unionists not only held them, but also practised them. The business mystics might have gone to these workmen to learn what morality is; since there can be no morality without practical obligations.

One of my first surprises then, after I joined the I.L.P. and came in contact with the trade unions, was the discovery that moral theories were not necessarily mere words, but could be taken quite seriously and a real attempt be made to put them into practice. The men who tried to practise them were not solemn or pious about them; they hardly ever spoke of them, and took them mostly for granted. But they had a tradition to keep up, and a tradition produces a delicate sense of honour; and they were pledged not to over-reach one another, and that is the basis of disinterested communication between human things. I had been amazed at some of the friendships I had known among my old acquaintances; friendships in which natural affection and calculation were inextricably interwoven, and which were largely held together by the reciprocal giving away of good business tips in the expectation that better ones would be received in return. These men constantly talked of their own business: the workmen talked of their union or of this or that change which affected industry or society, and their conversation was consequently far more interesting, for nothing could be more wearisome than dialogues consisting of: "Do you know how many orders I got to-day?" or: "Fancy how much our firm paid out in wages last Saturday!" which I have overheard a thousand times in the third-class carriages of Glasgow suburban trains, carried on by animated young men.

I am speaking of the trade unions twenty-odd years ago, not as they must be now that the semi-stoppage of industry and the pressure of capitalists have weakened them. If there had existed a statesman of sufficient disinterestedness at that time, he could have made these men and their unions the basis of a new society, for nowhere else would he have found such incorruptibility, or such a sincere desire to secure the general good. They had virtues on which such a man could have absolutely depended; they were strongly organised; and they had a discipline which they had themselves created. If a single policy un-ambiguously embodying the good of society had been put before them, they would have responded to it, and they would have had sufficient strength, with such a lead, to carry it through. A great number of these men are now living in semi-starvation on the dole; their sons, who might have carried on the tradition which they created, do not know what work or responsibility or discipline is; their unions barely contrive to remain in existence. If Capitalism manages finally to smash these unions, it will be a loss to civilisation greater than the loss that would be brought about by another war.

There were many among these men who spent all their hard-won evenings in working for their unions or for Socialism. They did this without expecting or receiving any reward. They started classes, spoke at meetings or sold "literature," as it was called; kept their members together; and attended to the business side of their branches. Some of them believed that Socialism would come in their time; the majority that it would not come until after their death. The practical historical result of their work was the Labour Party, and the elevation of Mr. J. H. Thomas and Mr. J. Ramsay Macdonald. In integrity of character and grasp of the real problems of the time often far above their leaders, they went on doing the tasks which they saw had to be done, and refusing the temptations which were offered them. They saw before them the life of a workman; that is, a life which could never escape into riches or even into moderate comfort. They embraced that life without a thought of rising from it except along with all their fellow-workmen. If such devotion and fidelity are not to be admired, then all our ideas of morality are mistaken.

There were others who studied philosophy and literature, and tried to understand the past. Among them were men of first-class intelligence, who, given a better opportunity, would have been heard of in the world. I have met among them Hegelians, Schopenhauerians, Spencerians, and even Nietzscheans; and the one thing one could generally depend upon in them was that they knew their subject and had served a regular apprenticeship to it, just as they did to the trades they followed. Occasionally one came across scatter-brained readers among them, who hopelessly jumbled up all the knowledge they had acquired and used it merely for display. But these were a small minority: the discipline of learning a trade and the exactitude required to practise it were in their bones, and when they took up a subject they set themselves to master it as if it were a handicraft. More of them turned to philosophy and science than to literature; I think naturally. I am trying to give some impression of the actual human beings who are hidden behind statistics of unemployment; I do not claim that the men I have been speaking of form a majority of them; but I have no doubt whatever that they are among them. What reparation can be offered to these men by society, for which they have worked unselfishly, and without considering their own advantage?

VI

I have no intimate acquaintance with the upper-classes of Glasgow (that is, the rich, for the terms there are equivalent), and have come in contact with them only at a few public receptions. I can only speak from these.

Nobody will ever understand Glasgow who does not realise that it is a city which has risen to wealth with enormous rapidity. People often complain that in the world generally invention outruns the ability of human beings to adapt themselves to it and to use it for the right ends. In a rapidly growing city the same thing happens with wealth; a number of people become rich in a very short time without any notion of how to spend their money even with ordinary selfish taste. This seems to have happened on a large scale in the United States before the present depression; and in its combination of riches and tastelessness upper-class Glasgow is very like the United States. The receptions I have mentioned might have been given in some Western American town where there had been a gold rush ten years before, since which the successful speculators and their wives and families had been busily reading books of etiquette.

But as I can speak with no exact knowledge of the rich of Glasgow, I shall give instead a short poem which took shape during my journey through the industrial regions, and arose from a sense of the violent contrasts that I saw on every side. The only excuse I give for it is that contrast can be more briefly expressed in verse than in prose, and can thus form a synopsis of a complex scene, otherwise difficult to put into words.

The women talk, tea-drinking by the fire
    In the back parlour. The rose afternoon
Stiffens out in the street to fog and mire.
    The blood-red bullying West confronts the moon.

The house-tops, sharpening, saw into the sky.
    Factory sirens wail and Rest is born,
A clockwork centipede that lumbering by
    Decorates heaven with silhouettes of horn.

Incandescent burners' arctic glare
  Strikes dead a thousand families as they sit
At high tea in the tenements. The air
  Takes at the tidal corner of the street

The hundred-horse-power pub's wave-shouldering
    boom
  And thickened voices babbling Judgement Day.
At the big house the Owner waits his doom
  While his Rhine-maiden daughters sit and play

Wagner and Strauss. Beneath the railway bridge
  In patient waxwork line the lovers stand.
Venus weeps overhead. Poised on the ridge
  The unemployed regard the Promised Land.

There are, of course, humane and intelligent people
among the rich of Glasgow, just as there are in every
class; it would be absurd to deny it. But if one considers them *as a class* one cannot honestly ignore certain
things, and particularly what may be called their geographical position in society. They are rich in the
midst of poverty, and their riches are built on a
foundation of poverty. Their money is made out of
coal, iron, shipbuilding, and various similar things.
The coal-miner, the iron-worker and the shipyard
labourer are poor. Yet it is a popular fiction that such
facts are merely economic and can be confined to one
sphere, and that they have no influence on the moral
character, the better thoughts and feelings and habits

of the rich. That cannot be the case. Wealth accumulated in such a way does not merely give its possessors the opportunity to lead a more free and comfortable life; it brings all sorts of drawbacks with it. It brings, for instance, the extraordinary conventions which every successful class erects for itself and insists on living within. These conventions are in the last resort barriers set up to shut it off as completely as possible from the classes beneath it. Though in appearance as irrational as the taboos of savage tribes, the quite practical basis of such customs lies in the desire, or rather the necessity, of the rich to close themselves off from the poor, or in other words to ignore the source from which their comfort and elegance are derived. Everybody who lives a little more comfortably than the poorest of all has to exercise this customary repression almost continuously, though for the most part he is not aware of it. Accordingly the rich have psychologically a far greater burden to bear than the poor; ostentation is one of the most obvious means of blinding themselves to it; and in this way perhaps the lives of the Glasgow rich can be explained, as well as their behaviour on public occasions.

VII

In spite of all these contrasts of wealth and poverty, the people who live in the rich and slum-ridden city of Glasgow have an underlying resemblance which, though not crucial, is yet very clear. To set out to define that resemblance would be an impossible and probably useless task. If one wanted a rough-and-ready generalisation to express the difference between a Glasgow man and an Edinburgh man, one might say that every Edinburgh man considers himself a little better than his neighbour, and every Glasgow man just as good as his neighbour. The attitude in both cases is competitive with a difference; which is represented by the presence in Edinburgh of a fairly old tradition that recognises distinctions of social rank, and in Glasgow of a purely competitive standard, whose axiom for many decades has been that the best results are obtained by everybody getting the most he can for himself in the general scramble. The implicit philosophy of an Edinburgh man is rank and privilege; of a Glasgow man equality. Actually these philosophies are fictions. The rank and privilege which the Edinburgh man worships is a mere popular mirage, these things no longer having the palpable meaning which they had two or three centuries ago, when a lord possessed more than a title and the rents from his estates. The equality which the Glasgow man asserts hardly exists at all, since there is no longer, if there ever was, an opportunity for every man to become rich. The ambition of the Edinburgh man is to win a position of public esteem, with a title if possible attached to it, combined with free entry into genteel society. The ambition of the Glasgow man is ample money, a big house in Kelvinside or Pollokshields, and all the other outward signs that he is a man of wealth. The Edinburgh vices are snobbery and gentility; the Glasgow ones tasteless ostentation and materialism. The sins of Edinburgh can be committed without very great expense, therefore, for even people with modest means can be snobbish and genteel; consequently these sins are fairly widespread in Edinburgh. Glasgow's sins are costly; one needs some initial capital to indulge in them; the result is that they are confined within a relatively small class: the rest of the population having no choice but to dream of them or jeer at them. The independent spirit of Glasgow predisposes it to the latter alternative more often than the former; but in the lower middle classes one may still find many devout dreamers.

A sadder distinguishing characteristic of the Glasgow man (and it cuts across all classes) is the mark that has been visibly impressed upon him by Industrialism, in the lineaments of his face and the shape and stature of his body. If one were set down in the middle of Glasgow without knowing what town one was in and without seeing a single factory or slum, one would know by looking at the people passing that one was in an industrial city. Certainly one would see many re-markable and eloquent faces, from which one could read more perhaps than from the polite masks of Edin-burgh; but a great number of them would show that characteristic distortion which one finds in industrial regions, and there alone. The mixture of races in Glasgow might have been fortunate enough in itself, being partly Lowland, partly Highland, and partly Irish; drawn, that is to say, from regions which produce men of good and sometimes beautiful physique. Thrown together in Glasgow amid completely different conditions, these men and women have suffered a violent transformation, and the characteristic products of their marriage to the Industrial System, their residence in the crucible, are squat and lumpy but very powerful physical types, and small, neat and agile ones. These types are perhaps the most fit to survive in an industrial civilisation; authorities on race, who are, however, probably the most undependable of all authorities, have asserted it. At any rate, such types can be found in great numbers in all classes in Glasgow, and give a special character to Glasgow crowds. Yet in spite of the change which they have suffered in their very physical frame, or perhaps partly because of it, there are more interesting faces to be found in Glasgow crowds than anywhere else, probably, in Scotland. The faces I am particularly thinking of give the impression of having passed through a prolonged test resembling some mysterious illness, from which they have emerged with their humanity and goodness intact. One sees such faces sometimes among the physically deformed; it is very strange and moving to see them among men and women physically vigorous. Sitting in Glasgow theatres, I have often been astonished by a sudden glimpse of some man's or woman's face with this particular look, which was like an unconscious revelation.

One's impressions of a people are bound to be incomplete and biassed, that is, determined by what one looks for in them; and to correct my own view I am going to take the liberty of quoting Mr. George Blake's brief analysis of the Glasgow people in his excellent book, *The Heart of Scotland*. "It may be confidently maintained," he says, "that here is the liveliest community in Scotland. This fantastic mixture of racial strains, this collection of survivors from one of the most exacting of social processes, is a dynamo of confident, ruthless, literal energy. The Glasgow man is downright, unpolished, direct, and immediate. He may seem to compare in that respect with the Aberdonian, but in him there is none of that queer Teutonic reserve, which is so apt to affect human intercourse with the native of Buchan. That he is a mighty man with his hands, the world knows and acknowledges; that he is nearer the poet than his brothers in the other cities is less obvious, but equally true. He has the 'furious' quality of the Scot in its most extreme form. He can be terribly dangerous in revolt and as terribly strong in defence of his own conception of order. He hates pretence, ceremonial, form—and is at the same time capable of the most abysmal sentimentality. He is grave—and one of the world's most devastating humorists."

Mr. Blake adds that these observations apply mainly to the Glasgow working man. They give a different picture of him from the one I have tried to give. If the two pictures could be combined, the result might be a more or less objective portrait of the Glasgow workman. "Downright, unpolished, direct, and immediate" certainly describes one side of him very well. Whether he is "nearer the poet" than other workmen, I could not say. He is certainly a mighty man with his hands, or was at one time. But I do not think that, singly or collectively, he is "a dynamo of confident, ruthless, literal energy," nor that it would be a good thing if he were. "Literal," it seems to me, is very good indeed, and here Mr. Blake has put his finger on an essential quality of the Clyde workman, the quality which makes him face the economic facts of society and wish to change them. "Dynamo" I don't much like, and "ruthless," I am certain, is quite wrong. Essentially the Glasgow workman is kindly and humane, with a real depth of humanity which transcends class distinctions, and is gathered from experience, mostly of hardship. It is a common fiction that humanity of this kind can be united in the same man with "ruthless" energy. Actually the man of ruthless energy sets himself to acquire a certain humanity of disposition, so that he may enjoy that warm sense of contact with other men which is often necessary to him. But that is a different matter; "humanity" then is a sort of compensation, an auxiliary, not a fundamental attribute; and it is always tinged with sentimentality. The humanity of the Glasgow workman is practical; and it is made quite real and unambiguous by the fact that he is, generally speaking, faithful to his class, and so has no use for "ruthless" energy, which is a weapon used by ambitious men to achieve success under conditions of unbridled competition. I have stopped so long at this one epithet of Mr. Blake's because it seems to me the only misleading one he uses, and because, apart from it, his portrait of the Clyde workman is an admirable one. There are certainly a great number of people in Glasgow with ruthless energy, but they are mainly to be found, I think, among the climbing middle classes and the men who have risen to wealth "by their own efforts," as the popular but misleading saying goes.

VIII

I have lingered for a long time in Glasgow, and yet I feel that I have given a very inadequate idea of its actual being as a community. Glasgow contains such a number of things: thousands of families living in harmony or in dissension, comfortably or poorly, in anything from one small room to twenty large ones: slums, villas and turreted mansions, varying in comfort, but alike in ugliness: factories, at work or silent: socialist societies and Y.M.C.A.s: churches, Catholic chapels and Orange halls: cinemas, dance-halls, tearooms and hotel lounges: literary societies: brothels: graveyards: trains and tram-cars where a whole population seems to be in migration: Labour Exchanges with queues waiting before the doors: streets of prostitutes: young men waiting for young women at a thousand

corners: football-matches: gymnasiums: Salvation Army
bands: fathers and mothers beating their children in
cold suburban parlours: bands of misguided or
desperate youths, who call themselves "The Norman
Conks," or by some other name, roaming about the
slums: professors: drinking clubs: street fights: black-
coated congregations dispersing from a thousand
churches, Catholic, Protestant, Baptist, Wesleyan,
Unitarian: unemployed men walking about in a
vacuum represented by one or two or five or ten years:
boxing-matches and theosophical lectures: luxurious
shops and shebeens: curtains discreetly raised and
lowered in suburban streets: bun-fights: Band of Hope
concerts: bridge drives: law-courts: schools: prisons:
official receptions: and a thousand things more which
paralyse the mind when it tries to number them. A
modern city is strictly inconceivable. Consequently I
have kept very largely to the economic side of Glasgow
life, because it is the essential one: the other aspects of
modern towns have become journalism. I actually intended at one point to say something about the
churches, and in particular about the furious clashes
between Orangemen and Catholics which fill the cells
of the lock-ups after every St. Patrick's Day. But these
things do not matter; they have only a fictitious importance; and to try to understand an Orangeman's
state of mind in any case would not only be extraordinarily difficult, but also quite profitless, for the
Orange superstition is surely one of the most insensate
of existing superstitions, and also one of the most un-

interesting. Unfortunately the Orange demonstrators and marchers belong mainly to the working class, just as the Catholic ones do. This feud causes a great deal of trouble, and has not even the excuse of being justified by interest. It is sheer inane loss: a form of hooliganism under the cover of something too silly even to be called an idea. But in the final count it comes to almost nothing. The fundamental realities of Glasgow are economic. How is this collapsing city to be put on its feet again?

CHAPTER V

THE HIGHLANDS

THE surroundings of Glasgow are beautiful, especially to the north, where the Highlands begin. A good many miles of the level ground lying between Glasgow and the hills have been covered during the past two decades with new suburbs, some of them, such as Knightswood, amounting to little towns. The houses in these new suburbs are mostly of the same pattern; that is, compact little boxes divided in two, with a door in each division from which a tiny strip of garden unrolls itself. These boxes are certainly more comfortable to live in than the old-fashioned tenements of twenty or thirty years ago; but they are extraordinarily unattractive, and also have a curious paper or cardboard-like appearance, as if they were stage properties belonging to some huge travelling company, which will one day be packed up and taken away to an enormous store-room. They do not seem to be attached to the landscape, or to have any other relation to it; and set end to end for miles they never make anything that resembles a street. They are curiously hypothetical, in fact; and one cannot help feeling that the people in them are temporary settlers, or tribes on the trek to some unknown destination. These colonies are deserted during the day by their men-folks; for an unemployed man could not afford to live in them. What the lives of the stranded women can be like in these settlements that are neither town nor country nor country town, it is impossible to imagine. It must be healthier than existence in a street of tenements, certainly; and the idea of building these suburbs sufficiently far from the centre of the town to provide fresh air for their dwellers was an excellent one. But it has been carried out with a comprehensive lack of imagination. These suburbs are no worse really than most of the suburbs that unevenly sprawl out of London on every side over the country; they have the same awkward intrusive air, as if they had pushed out farther than they intended, and were dismayed at finding themselves among fields. Beyond them to the north there is very fine country, and in a few miles one can be in the Highlands.

To the south of the town there are still twenty miles or so of fine moorland, which is shrinking fairly fast, but will be there, one feels, for many a day yet. To the west is the Clyde and the Valley of the Clyde, hilly on the north side, comparatively flat on the south, and on the estuary Port Glasgow and Greenock comfortably stink and rot, two of the dirtiest and ugliest towns in Scotland, with a natural position second only to Dundee, which is the dirtiest and ugliest of all. Beyond Greenock is Gourock, a summer resort, and opposite, on the Highland side, is a whole row of watering-places. From a hill to the north-east of Gourock one can see, on a spring or autumn evening, the lights of a dozen deserted summer resorts strung in little clusters and constellations along the banks of the Clyde: an extraordinarily pretty sight. If one could fly down the Clyde some night one would see scores of those pretty little constellations, all of them, after one had passed Greenock, involuntarily advertising holiday resorts. The life of Glasgow threw them off, and shot them farther and farther as time went on, till they now string the whole coast of Ayrshire from north to south. They have all something of their first cause in them, and through them Glasgow stretches out until, on the beach of Machrihanish, it faces the Atlantic Ocean.

I have been to most of these holiday resorts at one time or another, and for a year I lived in one of them. They are very like English places of the same kind. Some are blatant, some discreet: the first being well furnished with various entertainments, the latter small and devoid of them. These places have an extremely business-like air, like all pleasure resorts; but they have also a character of their own, and they are set in beautiful or charming surroundings. They are most of them "downright, unpolished, direct, immediate," to use Mr. Blake's words about Glasgow, and are honest towns of pleasure where the holiday-maker is expected to pay, but where he gets something substantial in return: the quantity of entertainment in such places as Dunoon and Rothesay is unstinted.

During my stay in Glasgow I went for a day's sail

down the Clyde with an old friend, and saw for the first time for many years all those familiar places approaching and receding as the boat ploughed on. It was a warm sunny day; the boat was filled with family parties of all sizes and shapes, and the piers and beaches were dotted with summer dresses which looked like irregularly planted rows of blossoming trees. Against the green, wooded, hilly background the effect was extraordinarily cheerful. As the firth widened and the fine mountainous outline of Arran drew near, changing continually as it did so, these gay little clumps fell away, and one could feel already the uncompromising melancholy of the Highlands. We left the boat at Campbeltown and got into a bus bound for Machrihanish, which lies at the opposite side of the narrow isthmus and looks straight out on the Atlantic. Machrihanish is one of the small and discreet holiday resorts, but as a town or rather a rickle of boarding-houses and hotels scattered at sixes and sevens over the low sandy ground (for that is all that it is), it is as tasteless and ugly as it could be. But its situation is magnificent, and looking out to sea even on a calm summer's day one can feel the full power of the Atlantic. Northward lie Islay and the fine Island of Jura with its two beautiful rounded hills which are called the Paps of Jura: they are like the magnificent breasts of some giantess lying outstretched on the ocean-bed. The unambiguity of these two hemispheres rising from the level plain of the sea adds a touch of human pathos to their majesty, and evokes with peculiar force the feeling that everyone must have had at moments in looking at nature: that it is a dumb living thing which has suffered for long ages an unjust but ordained imprisonment. The more strongly the forms of nature suggest some human association, the more deeply does one have this sense—whether real or illusory—of the imprisonment of nature. Such feelings are always mingled with sadness. I wanted to preserve some memento of them and went over to a stationary booth to buy a post-card of the Paps of Jura.

Gentility may spring from a misdirected or thwarted natural sensibility as well as from social fear or snobbishness, and the Highlanders are a peculiarly sensitive people. Machrihanish is an artificial eruption on a Highland shore where it is difficult for a Highlander to know what the social and moral code is. The two hills are there in any case for anyone to look at if he wishes. To come to the point, I could not buy nor beg a single picture post-card of the Paps of Jura. At last I managed to find a post-card with the legend: "Machrihanish, with a distant view of the Jura Hills," a triumph of trick photography in which by some inexplicable manipulation of perspective two tiny noncommittal almost invisible mounds were shown in the extreme right-hand corner. I bought this post-card and still treasure it.

One can feel the enchantment of the Highlands by taking a few steps out of Glasgow to the north or the north-west; and that seems at first one of the strangest things about it. The natural explanation is that

Glasgow is only the extreme fringe of a whole sea of grime and dirt extending eastwards almost to within sight of Edinburgh. To the north-west of Glasgow this sea washes against the hills and in between them until it is spent.

But it was to the east that I had to go now, between pocked fields through which iron-coloured brooks sluggishly oozed, and where stringy gutta-percha bushes rose from sward that looked as if it had been dishonoured by some recondite infamy. I noticed that as I drove through the defaced and suffering patches of country which still persist between Glasgow and Hamilton and Airdrie and Motherwell, no scents from the hedges and fields streamed into the open car. They had borne me company on my journey almost all the way to Glasgow; they rose to meet me again as soon as I was past the industrial belt, refreshing and sweetening the air. But it was as if in this region nature no longer breathed, or gave out at most the chill dank mineral breath of coal and iron. The air itself had a synthetic taste, the taste of a food substitute, and seemed to be merely an up-to-date by-product of local industry. The forlorn villages looked like dismembered parts of towns brutally hacked off, and with the raw edges left nakedly exposed. The towns themselves, on the other hand, were like villages on a nightmare scale, which after endless building had never managed to produce what looked like a street, and had no centre of any kind. One could not say that these places were flying asunder, for there was no visible sign of anything holding them together; the houses merely stood side by side; of every shape and size, they crowded upon each other so hard that they seemed to be squabbling in a slatternly, apathetic, dejected way for their places. But they had no relation to each other except this; arranged in any order one felt that they never would amount to a town. They were merely a great number of houses jumbled together in a wilderness of grime, coal-dust and brick, under a blackish-grey synthetic sky.

Round these bloated and scabbed villages there are ranges of slag-heaps, miniature mountain ranges which, though they have no more connection with the green fields round them than the villages themselves, give one the illusion of being geological in formation, so convincing are their contours. These black slag peaks and valleys make up a toy landscape which is not enchanting like the toy landscape of the Tweed Valley, but dwarf-like and sinister, suggesting an immeasurably shrivelled and debased second-childhood. They also suggest sand and ash castles and mud pies done on an enormous scale, and call to mind naïve childhood and idiot senility so expressively at one and the same time, that one forgets that they are mere products of ingenious and unlimited greed. I saw young men wandering in groups among these toy ranges, and the sight suddenly recalled to me the wood-cuts in *The Pilgrim's Progress* which I had read as a boy; perhaps because this scene really seemed to be more like an allegorical landscape with abstract figures than a real landscape with human beings. The abstruse ugliness of this black iron and coal region is such a true reflection of the actual processes which have gone on in it during the last hundred years that the landscape has acquired a real formal and symbolical significance which one cannot find in the slatternly chaos of Glasgow. Some painters are bound to be attracted by it, I should say, though none is likely ever to live in it or to be born in it.

A little beyond Motherwell I came upon the tiny village of Carfin with its Grotto, which I had been told to look out for. This place of pilgrimage was created some years ago by the Roman Catholic Church in honour of Sister Thérèse of the Child Jesus, a young French girl of great piety who died of consumption in 1897. The Grotto covers a good deal of ground and contains a heterogeneous collection of rock-gardens, lawns, shrines, images of Christ and the Virgin, which are rather confusing to one's eye on a hot summer's day. The greater part of the actual labour on this shrine, apart from the planning and the statuary, was done voluntarily by miners and railwaymen. I have heard people who know more than I do about plastic art criticising its arrangement; nevertheless, it appeared to me the only palpable assertion of humanity that I came across in the midst of that blasted region. Father Taylor, who was largely instrumental in having the sanctuary begun and completed, and now watches over it, deserves to be honoured by the people of these towns. I could vouch from my own experience that the place, with its green lawns, its flowers, its little streams winding through their rocky mazes, its shrines and statues, had a power of communicating peace which is extraordinarily rare in the modern world. There were very few visitors to it when I was there, that was in the late forenoon of a very hot summer's day; and the only people I spoke to were two old Irishwomen who asked me some question or other about the Grotto which I could not answer. They rattled on cheerfully about Glasgow, where they lived, hoping for a time that I was Irish too, but finally arriving at the fact that I was not. Thereupon they sympathised with me, poured a few pious but kindly blessings over me, and left me to myself. The last I saw of them they were kneeling side by side on the warm grass before one of the many statues.

This sanctuary is such an extraordinary place to find in such surroundings that a short history of it may be interesting. I have gathered from Father Taylor's little book on it, *The Carfin Grotto,* the following facts. It was built in imitation of the Grotto at Lourdes and dedicated on the first Sunday of October, 1922, the feast of Our Lady of the Rosary. The feast of the Rosary coincided that year with the silver jubilee Sunday of Sister Thérèse of the Child Jesus, who in life had named herself the "Little Flower of Jesus." Before she entered the order of the Carmelites at the age of fifteen, Sister Thérèse was Marie Thérèse Martin. She was born in Alençon in 1873 and died in 1897 at the age of twenty-four, her last words being: "My God,

I love Thee!" She declared on her death-bed: "I shall spend my Heaven doing good upon earth . . . I shall let fall a shower of roses." Before she died she wrote an account of her life, which breathes a beautiful and pure spirit, and is filled with an ardent love of all living things. This book has been finely translated by Father Taylor, and has sold, I believe, by hundreds of thousands.

Since her death Sister Thérèse has had an extraordinary influence. "North and South America," says Father Taylor, "love her even more passionately than does her own land of France. Such is her influence in heathen lands, that over two hundred bishops and prefects in those countries petitioned Pius XI to constitute her patroness of the Foreign Missions on an equal footing with the great missionary, St. Francis Xavier." Her influence has also been shown in more modest ways. "She brought the Rev. Mr. Grant, of the United Free Church of Scotland, into the Catholic Church" and "She has just been instrumental in converting the distinguished writer, Miss Sheila Kaye-Smith (Mrs. Fry), and in leading the Rev. Vernon Johnson from Canterbury to Rome, the heaviest blow to the Anglo-Catholic movement since that dealt by Robert Hugh Benson." "In the spring of 1923," says Father Taylor, "it was she who drew to the Grotto the vast crowds of that summer—over a quarter of a million pilgrims within three months."

Now to turn to Carfin itself. In July, 1920, a group from Carfin took part in the Scottish pilgrimage to

Lourdes, and decided on returning to erect a small grotto on some ground opposite the church. Carfin is a mining village. It is a bleak and ugly enough little place, but its name, which Father Taylor says is of Gaelic origin, apparently means "beautiful residence." The great majority of the population is Irish, with an admixture of Lithuanian. The village is quite a small one, and the fact that a knoll close by contains the ruins of an ancient sanctuary does not seem an adequate explanation for the erection of a new one in such an unlikely place. Cardinal Bourne, in an address given at the Grotto in 1924, asked in his usual rhetorical style "Why Carfin?" and went on, "Why Nazareth?" Father Taylor is more reasonable on this point. "Perhaps one may ascribe the choice, in part at least," he says, "to the faith of the three hundred volunteers who have toiled at the shrine." But then he continues, less reasonably, perhaps: "We must reckon, too, with the promise from the nuns of the Carmel of Lisieux, from the surviving sisters of St. Thérèse, that the Little Flower would multiply the pilgrims to Carfin, and so prove her passionate love for Mary, the mother of Christ. Intercession is also made for it in Uganda, in India, in China; at Loreto and Genazzano; in ancient Chartres, at Notre Dame des Victoires, and by special command of its Bishop—at the Grotto of Lourdes itself; as well as in countless centres of devotion nearer home."

If some of these quotations should sound ironical to a Protestant reader, it is without any intention of mine; for the Grotto is too interesting as a piece of contemporary history, and too clearly the creation of a sincere faith, to be treated with superficial sarcasm. The Grotto was opened in October, 1922. By next year water from its well had begun to be carried away for the use of the sick. "On June 10th, 1923," says Father Taylor, "the event happened which focused on Carfin the attention of the Scottish Press, east and west, not for a day, but for weeks. . . . The Carfin Grotto was hailed as the Scottish Lourdes. Mrs. Holmes was cured after a visit to the Grotto . . . and the secular journals circulated the news far and wide." And he quotes from the *Edinburgh Evening Despatch:* "To stand in the main street of Carfin, and to watch the people streaming into the Grotto . . . is an experience not readily to be forgotten. Parties travelled yesterday from all parts of the Midlands of Scotland. From two o'clock the main street was one continuous bustle. In the Grotto was a long queue, six or eight deep, waiting to drink from the well. Many carried bottles, and these were filled from the pool." The number of pilgrims went on increasing. "The attendance on the last Sunday of July," says Father Taylor, "was estimated at 70,000. At times the queue, four deep, moved slowly on for five hours before reaching the well." This increase of worshippers made it essential to enlarge the Grotto. The work was begun in January, 1924, and the enlarged Grotto reopened on Easter Monday that year. Since then the work of extension and embellishment has been going on fairly continuously, and almost entirely by voluntary labour. During this time pilgrimages from all over Scotland, and even from England and Ireland, have come to the Grotto, and the miraculous cure of Mrs. Holmes has been followed by several others.

These miraculous cures are very interesting, and have every appearance of credibility. The cure of Mrs. Holmes, which drew the attention of the Scottish newspapers to Carfin, is a good example. This old lady suffered from rheumatoid arthritis so badly that her hip-joint was pushed out of its place. The doctors told her that she need not expect to be cured. In June, 1923, when she was seventy-six, her friends assisted her to Carfin, where she said her prayers and drank from the well. On returning to her home in Coatbridge she slept deeply and found when she awoke that her hip-joint "had returned almost to its normal position," the pain had gone, and she could walk about freely. She showed her thanks to the Grotto by depositing her crutch there. She died a few years later of bronchitis.

In the same year a child was cured of eczema and another of blindness. Mrs. Bell, of Greenock, was miraculously cured of tuberculosis, and John M'Geehin, of Glasgow, of hernia. The story of Mr. William Findlay, of Aberdeen, is particularly interesting. About fifteen years before the cure he had a bad fall on the head which made him deaf. He went to the Grotto, and a priest touched his ears with a relic. This is his own description of what happened: "As I raised my hand to cross myself, I felt a crack in my head, as if someone had dealt me a blow on the back of the skull. I did not know what happened. When my wife, my son and I were coming away from the Grotto, I heard the crunching of the gravel, and when I stepped into the road I heard the motor-cars. The sound was terrifying to me and I felt dazed. As the train drew up at the halt I remarked to my wife that it was making a terrible noise. She looked surprised, and when we were seated I had to explain. That journey was the most wonderful in my life. For the first time in fifteen years I heard the rumble of the wheels and the chattering of the people. Indeed, I am not yet able to fall asleep at night until the tram-cars on the beach have stopped running." Nobody could call in doubt a story so circumstantial and so sincere as that. And the same can be said of the other miracles related in Father Taylor's little book.

I have told the story of the Grotto as objectively as possible, so as to let it speak for itself. It is, looked at from any point of view, an astonishing story. Here, in one of the most hideous stretches of country-side, in an industrial region festering with poverty and unemployment, a flourishing shrine has grown up in a few years, one of the causes of whose popularity is that it produces miraculous cures of quite ordinary ailments. Many of these ailments, moreover, it is clear from Father Taylor's little book, are directly produced by the working of the Industrial System in the middle of which this shrine stands. On the other hand, it has risen without the help of that system, and by means which are foreign to it; for the Grotto is the result of voluntary labour, the labour of poor men. The influence of a young French girl who died in 1897 has attracted pilgrims to it. Intercession for it is made in Africa, in Asia, and several countries in Europe. It is a part not only of Scotland but of a whole world of which most of Scotland knows nothing. It is as international as the industrial region that surrounds it, but in a completely different way. Obviously it has no relation to the vital and suffering life of present-day Scotland, for Scotland has a deeper and more widespread disease than rheumatoid arthritis or hernia, and a few miraculous cures can do nothing to alter its state; at best they make interesting reading. But that a place like the Grotto should manage to appear in a place like Carfin is astonishing, at the most moderate estimate.

After leaving Carfin I turned to the north instead of continuing through the black belt. As I neared Stirling I could see on my right a cloud of dense darkness, which showed where Falkirk lay round its furnaces. I decided I had had enough of this ravaged country, and as I drove into Stirling with its bright, solid, stylish country town air, I felt as if I had been wandering in a strange world and was back again in the Scotland I knew. I stopped for lunch at a hotel, and afterwards wandered through the pleasant streets, and watched from a height the fascinating labyrinthine curves of the slow Forth winding between meadows greener than I had seen for a long time. I looked at some of the old houses that climb crookedly up to the Castle on the rock, and found that, like the old tenements in almost all Scottish historical cities, they had largely degenerated into slums. From Stirling Castle one can get a more impressive prospect than from any other castle I have seen in Scotland. The Lowlands stretch behind you; the Highlands rise before you; and east and west for many miles coil the impossibly intricate silver windings and turnings of the Forth flowing through its level meadows. The sight almost dazed me after the sights I had seen; and it seemed strange that running streams should be clear and grass green.

I was so absorbed in such thoughts that I never thought of Wallace and Bruce and Bannockburn until, after driving across the Forth, I passed on the north side the Wallace Monument, a high tower in the ancient Scottish style which watches over the Forth and looks down towards Edinburgh. It was at Stirling Bridge that Wallace first defeated the English on a large scale, at Falkirk, a few miles away, that he was defeated in turn, and at Bannockburn, a few miles away on the other side of the town, that Bruce gained his famous victory. A battle is proceeding at present over the place where this victory was won. Two places lay claim to this honour; I have seen them both: one many years ago, the traditional field of Bannockburn, which was merely an ordinary field on a farm, and the other, quite recently, the modern field of Bannockburn, which is a public park of Stirling, the King's Park. I tried to imagine a battle being waged in either of these places, but was quite unsuccessful; it may be because places where men have thought or created things always leave some trace behind which makes it worth while to visit them, and places where men have fought leave nothing at all; or it may be because I have no vestige of what is called the military imagination, or because Stirling Bridge and Falkirk and even Bannockburn have now only a story-book reality. At any rate, the only image that Wallace could call up to me was that of an old carter in Glasgow whom I had known twenty years before. In his youth he had been a renowned ploughman; he was immensely broad in the shoulders, and his enormous hands still looked as if they were feeling for the stilts. After drinking for some time in silence he would flap his great hand on the counter of the public-house and roar: "Wallace, the hero o' Scotland!" If nobody paid any attention to this, he would drink for another half-hour and flap his hand on the counter again. Then he would look round and ask angrily: "D'ye ken what the English did to him, the dirty b——s? Libbed him!" After that he would growl to himself for a time over his beer, but then, as he grew merry, he would tell stories of his feats at ploughing-matches as a young man, and of his prowess with the women. When he got really drunk he would bellow out in a voice that had once been good an old song beginning:

"Fareweel, fareweel, my native hame."

He had no use for Burns; his hero was Wallace. There

was more of Scotland in him, I think, than in any other man I have ever met. He had been for more than twenty years a lorryman in the employment of a Glasgow beer-bottling factory, and lived in what was nearly a slum.

I made a stop for tea at a little village some distance from Perth, and on entering found a very different character, a young man of dark and foreign appearance who had passed me on the road in a magnificent car. I found out that he was a traveller for a well-known foreign firm; but he himself was a talkative Londoner who had very little good to say of Scotland, except for its scenery, upon which he had often camped out with his fiancée. They had done so the summer before in the north of Sutherlandshire, and when I asked him if it had not been rather cold he laughed at the idea and gave me an account of a modern camper's outfit which surprised me. He always carried with him, he said, instead of a sleeping bag a sort of pneumatic rubber mattress which could be rolled up in small compass and inflated by a tyre pump until one could rest upon it light as a feather several inches above the ground, secure from the damp. He had also an army of hot-water-bottles, a collapsible cocktail-shaker, and a very small travelling wireless set; and fortified by these he said he had had a splendid holiday. Being a man of such habits, he thought the Scottish people uncivilised, and was particularly impressed by the savagery of the lower classes in the towns, who, he said, made no attempt whatever to keep up appearances. He was a pleasant enough young man, but an extraordinary chatterbox, or seemed so to me after meeting so many Scots people. He had views on every single subject, from business to the persecuted Jews in Germany, and these views were all equally fluent, equally idle and equally without any relation to each other. He thought business was looking up and that the Jews deserved everything that came to them, and had the mind of a child, and a vocabulary made up of newspaper and business clichés. This type is not often to be found in Scotland, where everyone, however illiterate, has a distant knowledge of and respect for logic, and can generally give some reason for the beliefs that he holds; a fact that no doubt partly accounts for the ubiquity of argument in Scotland. This young Londoner, at any rate, produced an extraordinarily foreign impression sitting in that little Scottish village tea-room, surrounded by sober Scottish hills. He left before I did, for he had to interview several customers in Perth.

I stopped in Perth to buy a basket of strawberries, and pushed on to a remote part of Angus where I wished to see a married couple, old friends of mine, who were running a farm there. After supper they began telling me about the lives of their neighbours, mostly farmers and farm labourers. I did not know much about life on a modern farm in Scotland, although I was brought up on one, and so I listened attentively.

According to my friends there has been a great

change in Scottish country life during the last twenty or thirty years. Before that the servants on a farm were more or less members of a family and ate in the kitchen at one long table along with their master and mistress. In the larger farms this has now completely changed, and my friends put this down partly to the increased commercialisation of farming, and partly to such mechanical devices as the motor-car, the use of which automatically translates the man who owns it into a different world from other people. Once both master and servant were penned within a relatively small world represented by the farm they lived on and a few neighbouring farms. Their sole concern was with the ground and how it could be tilled in a workmanlike way, and this task bound them together. But now, with the vast increase of means of communication, and the consequent generalisation of every activity, the farmer's work has been specialised in one direction and the servant's work in another until they have very little in common. The farmer has become a sort of book-keeper, the servant a mere labourer. This is one reason for the break-up of the old unity. The other is that modern contrivances allow the farmer, whether very prosperous or not, to live a life quite different from the life of the people he employs. His house is fitted with the same conveniences as a town flat, and once he is inside it he might be in Kelvinside or any other better-class suburb of a Scottish city. His car can take him to the theatre or the cinema in the nearest big town. The result is that he is becoming more and more urbanised, and losing more and more his traditional country way of looking at things.

But this is only one side of the picture. For the farm labourer can afford none of these town amenities, and so his life has remained very much what it has been for a hundred years. On Saturday afternoon he can take a bus to the nearest town; but he cannot afford a wireless set, far less a car, and, cut off from his old community of interest with his master, he has sunk to the status of an almost outcast class. The average wage of a married farm labourer in the district where my friends lived was twenty-five shillings a week, with a free house of two or three rooms, and an allowance of meal and milk. Some farmers pay only twenty-one shillings a week. Out of such sums the great part of the food, all the clothes, and all the fuel of a family have to be provided for. The result is that the farm-labouring class live in a state of permanent serfdom almost as absolute as if the farmers owned them. If a labourer falls ill he has the benefit of his Health Insurance, but his wages and meal and milk allowance are often docked if he lies off work, and he has to foot the doctor's bill for any other sickness in his household. His wife and family are expected to help with the work of the farm when needed, for which they get a small extra pay. When they have to lie in the women very often do not send for a doctor, but call in a neighbour to see them through their time of labour. They often conceal their illnesses for fear of being sent to some hospital in a distant town, leaving their children uncared for. There was in this district a peculiar horror of hospitals, which was due, my friends thought, to the fact that most women refused to go to one until it was too late, so that a great number of them never returned. The life of farm labourers on a bad farm can be made wretched beyond description. These serfs work for their masters on a yearly tenure, and when the annual feeing day comes round the farmer's whim, if he is a bad master, is all that they have to depend upon for another year's livelihood. I was told that for days before that many a family lives in a state of pitiable misery, not knowing what is to become of them, and willing to do anything to show their pathetic submissiveness. There are many farmers who treat their servants so well that this yearly anxiety is spared them. There are a few whose labourers live and die in their service, quite contented with their lot, and knowing that their livelihood is secure. But the status of a farm labourer, whether he is well or ill-treated, is too like slavery to be agreeable; for it is wellnigh impossible for him to escape from the poor, hard, narrow and subservient existence he is condemned to, except by emigration, and since the war even emigration has become a false hope. Apart from their dole of meal and milk, he and his family live on the cheap and substitute foods that they buy from the vans. In this hard existence the men are better off than the women, for they are out in the fields all day, away from the visible presence of poverty. Many of the children look half starved. The women lose their looks almost with the first child they bear.

I asked my friends why such a state of things should exist in a fertile agricultural district where the farms seemed to be well run and prosperous; but they were not able to give any clear explanation. Farming, they told me, was not very profitable, and many of the farmers could not afford to pay their men any better. They were convinced that something was generally wrong with farming, or with the relation of farming to the rest of the economy of production; for even if one used the latest and most scientific methods of cultivation, and made the soil produce all that it could, the return in actual profit was never very great. The stories they told me of the farm labourer's life, of women dying in childbirth because they could not afford to call in a doctor, or stubbornly working on until they collapsed because they were terrified of being taken away to hospital, spoiled my enjoyment of the country-side, which in that district is rich and fertile, with pleasant woods and sheltered banks covered with masses of wild flowers.

I left next afternoon to cut back into the main Highland road for Inverness. I reached Dunkeld in the evening and decided to put up there. The hotel I stopped at had an air of having come down in the world, and the waiters a permanent lugubrious look, as if they were blaming mankind for the lack of customers. In such places the arrival of a single visitor is more an insult than a matter for congratulation, and when the waiters, standing in a little group, caught sight of me as I entered the dining-room, I felt that their main feeling was disgust at my being only one: for it would have needed a party of twenty to dispel their sardonic disillusionment. One of them, a burly man of forbidding dignity, approached me and disapprovingly listened to my order, which was not a very long or elaborate one. He sighed as he went away, brought my beer and steak, and then, as if he assessed my order as a kind of disguised high tea, set down buttered toast and jam, and heaving another sigh returned in a few minutes with a plate of cakes, and a little later with cheese and biscuits. Out of all these things I made an excellent meal. Clearly there were not many people staying at the hotel; at a table at the other end of the long room three ladies were having high tea with fried sole, but otherwise the place seemed deserted. I wondered at this, for some time in the recent past the hotel must have been a popular one. I imagine that Dunkeld must have suffered one of those minor disasters that often come to holiday places. People went to it for the summer months in times when communication was not so easy as it is now, for Dunkeld is accessible and at the gateway to the Highlands. Now I fancy people make it a stop on their journey, and so, pretty as it is, it has acquired a somewhat derelict appearance. I wandered for some time along the banks of the Tay, which is quite narrow here, enquired whether I could get into the Cathedral, but found I was too late, for it was closed to visitors at eight, and retired early to bed, having admired Birnam Hill, a compact steep wooded bluff, from the distance.

I started rather late next morning and in a little while found myself definitely in the Highlands. I am not going to describe that beautiful country, so often described already, or catalogue the host of famous mountains that I passed on my way. The thing that impressed me most in the Highlands during my first day's run (apart from a small incident to which I shall come presently) was a thing which is common no doubt to all wild and solitary scenery: that is, the added value which every natural object acquires from one's consciousness that it has not been touched by the human will. The larch woods, the streams, all of them noisy and active here because of the slant at which they run, the little mounds of turf: all had an exhilarating freshness which is absent from more cultivated places, and seemed to exist completely in themselves, as if they were their own end. The brooks seemed freer, the trees more naturally grown, and the silence that they filled with their presence almost a conscious thing. It may be simply that when one is alone with a hundred square miles of solitary nature one begins to become aware of its life as an independent mode of being. At any rate this awareness, whatever its cause, is refreshing. It seemed to me that the few solitary figures whom I passed on the almost empty road had a different look on their faces from the people I had grown accustomed to, and were a different race. The scent of birch and the light tinkle of streams filled the air all the forenoon, making it something different from ordinary air, something along with which one inhaled the fine essence of the free things growing round about: there was in it also a tincture of rock.

All the morning the air was warm and light, but towards one o'clock huge clouds began to collect to the south among the mountain crests; they overtook me; the sky darkened for the first time since I had set out from Edinburgh; and the atmosphere grew sick and heavy, with a faint touch of wetness. By the time I reached Kingussie, a summer holiday resort among the Cairngorms, the sun had made a deep cleft among the clouds again, and the main street was like a long empty baking oven. After enquiring in a tobacco shop which was the most reasonably cheap hotel, I went there for lunch and found the large dining-room already filled, and pretty dark-haired Highland waitresses flying from table to table. There seemed to be a great number of Glasgow-like ladies of late middle age in the place, with faces of formidable determination, who sailed into the room like miniature battleships, and bore down on their chosen tables as if they were enemies to be ruthlessly broached. These matrons had something of the air of invaders, too, and seemed conscious that here they were in foreign waters, but also that, as they had paid for these seas by a private agreement, their presence was perfectly lawful. In their faces was that unscrupulous determination to enjoy themselves which is so common in people who are on the verge of old age, when the capacity for pleasure in outward things is about to shrink for ever. They flung themselves on their food with a greed which was touching and quite unconscious, and drove the waitresses as hard as they could, as if they took pleasure in setting this covey of pretty young girls in a ceaseless flurry of movement at their bidding. In such ways they enjoyed themselves so openly and scandalously that they made the younger people in the room look quiet and dejected. This demonstration, I felt, was probably repeated at every meal held in that huge dining-room. The men who attended these ladies were somewhat subdued. After the meal was over I found most of them in the lounge having a quiet smoke. There was one incident during lunch. Three severe middle-aged ladies entered and sat down at a table: they looked like schoolteachers. In a little while they began to fidget, and as this had no effect audibly complained. A waitress stopped apologetically at their table and spoke to them. They replied sharply and in unison, and a few minutes later left with loud complaints. I felt that I had seen a representative example of Scottish hotel life, and resumed my journey.

When I stepped into my car the sky had darkened again and the air in my face was cool and wet. The mountains had shrunk, and their sides were inky-blue against the greyish-blue of the thunder clouds. Presently large drops began to fall, and I could hear a faint rumble of thunder behind the wall of hills. I drove on for a little, enjoying the rain in my face.

Then with a long leap the thunder jumped the hills and seemed to be all around me. The rain beat down as if shot from the clouds in liquid bullets which fell with such force that they rebounded several inches from the road. I stopped the car, got out, and hurriedly pushed forward and secured the hood. The peals of thunder were coming fast now, and every one of them was flung about between the mountain peaks for quite a long time, producing an effect of a bombardment from every side. During my short stop a score of cars seemed to have passed me, racing at top speed to get out of the thunder zone. I had not noticed more than three or four on the whole route up to then; but now the road seemed to be alive, and the black glistening shapes rushing past one after another reminded me of a furious host of cockroaches scuttling away at some disturbance. I got into the car again and drove on. Suddenly, as I got up speed, the hood flew back over my head again, and the rain poured down solidly into the car. I stopped, got out, hauled forward the hood once more and firmly screwed it down. Then I settled myself in my seat and pressed the self-starter. Nothing happened; for the first time since I had begun my journey the little car refused to act. The thunder was louder than ever; cars were now racing past in hundreds; I got out in exasperation and began to tinker with the plugs, without knowing much about them. The car looked extraordinarily forsaken amid the pouring din, but the thunder was gradually rolling away to the north; I had seen only one or two flashes of lightning. Suddenly the storm was over and I was standing in a thin gentle rain, which did not seem so much to fall as to settle down in small feathery drops. The air was saturated with odours that rose all round in such a thick cloud that I felt I could almost touch it. The car stood contentedly by the side of the road. I got in, somewhat drenched, and pressed the self-starter. The engine responded at once.

I drove on through gentle rain which steadily grew thinner till it faded to a mere veil, a nothing; and in an hour's time I was able to unscrew the hood again and drive in the open air. Gradually the hills sank, fir-woods enclosed me on both sides, big country houses with winding red gravel drives appeared, then farms, and presently as I drove along a long straight road I found myself on a crest with the sea before me and far away the mountain peaks of Caithness. The sky was still covered by a thin curtain of cloud, but the light was perfectly limpid and pure; and outlined in it everything, far and near, was both soft and distinct, almost colourless and quite without shadow. The sea looked as clear as a great rain-pool and at the horizon ran away without a break into the sky.

As I drove down into Inverness I passed a by-road marked Culloden, but remembering my lack of instinct for battlefields I held straight on. Inverness gave me the impression I have always had on visiting it; that is, of being inconveniently crowded with vehicles of all kinds, most of them stationary. I reached it about five o'clock and asked the first man I met where

I could get tea. He directed me to a luxurious tea-room somewhat in the Princes Street style, but in better taste and with fewer subdued lights, where a great number of young people, all of them startlingly good-looking, were sitting. In my dusty and oily state I felt disinclined to intrude into such a place, but I did not want to go out again and search for another, and to see so many handsome people in one room was a pleasure which I had not had for a long time. Also I wanted to inhale the atmosphere of Highland life at first in this qualified solution before I came to the real thing, which I hoped to find in my later journeyings.

Even in that little bourgeois tea-room in Inverness I felt that I was in a different land from the one I had been wandering through till then. It is difficult to say why I should have felt this. My first impression was of something absent from the atmosphere, something to which I had become used in the tea-rooms of Edinburgh and Glasgow, and which I thought of as a sort of charged thundery heaviness composed of unresolved desire from which the lightning of an aggressive or a provocative glance might flash at any moment. The tea-room was furnished with subdued lights in the Lowland style, it was true, but they did not have the effect for which they were designed, that is to create a vague sensuous twilight in which the floating desire of a Calvinistic people might unfold in safety, making a profit for the proprietor. This device, which must be as old as venereal science itself, though undis-covered and unpopularised by the Scottish tea-room proprietor until less than half a century ago, simply did not work here; for the young men and women sat about like a well-bred company in a drawing-room where the blinds had been lowered to keep out the glare. There was in this atmosphere a strange lack of insistence, after Glasgow and Edinburgh, something contained and yet free, detached and yet spontaneous, which seemed so impervious to all desire to draw attention to itself that it conveyed a faint sense of defeat. I suddenly remembered a very strong impression I had had one still summer day in Monte Carlo during the weeks when the Casino was shut. The gardens were deserted, but on the benches a few constant visitors were idly sitting in the sun, visibly glad that they had found a refuge in that emptiness from the congested hell of gambling. As I sat watching these little groups of released souls Blake's lines came into my mind:

> "And through all eternity
> I forgive you, you forgive me."

I felt that I had strayed into a curious modern version of the isle of Avilion

> "Where falleth neither sleet nor snow nor any rain,"

and I had somewhat the same feeling, though less intensely, in that little tea-room in Inverness. I was to have it more strongly later on, when I reached the Western Highlands. There Avilion is overrun by tourists in kilts, but I always felt that underneath these decorations the old life went on unchanged or almost unchanged, though the tourist could no more see it than he could see a dream.

I wanted to spend the night in a smaller town than Inverness, so I turned the nose of the car westwards towards Beauly. It was a clear evening full of watery lights, and the surface of the long narrow firth along whose south bank the car ran had the full smoothness of water continuously flowing over a sluice. The black road glistened, and drops were still falling from the thick woolly branches of the firs, as if they were trying already to blot out a little of the summer. The houses and fields at the opposite side of the strait had the peculiar teasing intimacy of things which are both near and inaccessible, reawakening in my mind one of the most persistent illusions of childhood: that everything can be easily reached, no matter what obstacles may lie between one and it. In the wet light the near bank, the far one and the firth itself seemed to flow past with the transparent motion of water. Presently a thin soft rain began to fall, enhancing still more the watery softness of the landscape, the firth fell behind, and the road wound through wooded inland country.

It was still raining when I reached Beauly and found myself once more in a hotel. In this little town the pleasant sensations which I had begun to feel in Inverness grew stronger, and crystallised into a sense of having a great deal of time and space to do what I liked with, a common feeling in the Highlands. The room I was shown into was large and bright, and the main street on to which it looked out was about six times the width of an ordinary street, resembling more than anything else a continental market square set down in the country, with a few low houses to define with studied carelessness its outline. Why this street should have been built on such spacious lines I don't know: probably it is used or was once used as a weekly market for the farming community round about; in any case the effect is very pleasant. At the end of this wide street, abutting into it and producing still more convincingly the impression of a square, is a low red church which, I found out from the guide-book, "was founded in 1230 by Sir John Basset of Lovat for Cistercians from Val des Choux near Châtillon-sur-Seine" and was "handed over at the Reformation to the 6th Lord Lovat, whose descendants forfeited the estates." Probably the presence of this church determined the shape of the street which stretches in front of its gates, and makes it still look, in spite of its breadth, exactly what it ought to be. I spent a pleasant hour after the rain had stopped in wandering through the church and the churchyard looking at the tombs of the Clan of Mackenzie, and following from the inscriptions the mortal fortunes of families through three or four centuries, an occupation which gives existence a quietude and simplicity which it certainly does not have in reality.

The hotel dining-room, like most of the others I was to find in the Highlands, had its walls covered with pictures of all sorts of wild game, living or in the various postures of death that are produced by sport. Between the pictures the walls were alert with the stuffed heads of deer, furnished with antlers of every degree of magnificence. A friend of mine has a theory that these pictures of dying birds and wounded beasts are intended to whet the diner's appetite, and perhaps they did in the more lusty age of Victoria; but I found they had the opposite effect on me, and I had to keep my eyes from straying too often to them. In one particular hotel this idea was carried out with such thoroughness that the walls of its dining-room looked like a shambles, they presented such an overwhelming array of bleeding birds, beasts and fishes. To find these abominations on the walls of Highland hotels, among a people of such delicacy in other things, is peculiarly revolting, and rubs in with superfluous force the fact that this is a land whose main contemporary industry is the shooting down of wild creatures; not production of any kind but wholesale destruction. This state of things is not the fault of the Highlanders, but of the people who have bought their country and come to it chiefly to kill various forms of life. These intruders do not understand or regret the corrupting effect this must have on a race forced to accept this abnormal life as a vocation. Such a life is natural enough in nomad tribes who have never known the arts of civilisation; but in a civilised people it is so unnatural that it gives one a feeling of perversity.

The history of the clearances in the Highlands over

a century ago is well known, so I shall not say much about them. Thousands of crofters' families were evicted and their farms turned into sheep-runs, on the principle that sheep were more profitable than human beings. Crofters who protested or even begged for a few days' delay had their houses burned over their heads. Many died of exposure and starvation: the more fortunate escaped overseas to a life of exile. The chief excuse for this barbarous treatment of a helpless people was first of all economic: to turn their crofts into sheep-runs seemed more productive, and so the enlightened opinion of the day held it to be desirable. Mrs. Beecher Stowe, who could not have been an inhuman woman, was actually angry with the Highlanders for complaining of losing their homes.

Another excuse was that the crofters were lazy and improvident, and that their farms were so poor that they lived in a state of semi-starvation. That they were very near starvation some winters cannot be denied: but nevertheless they produced a race of men who were the admiration of Europe. There is a very interesting passage about them in Eckermann's conversations with Geothe. Talking about the people of Paris, Eckermann said that he had once seen in Napoleon's time an infantry battalion made up of Parisians, but all of them looked so small and thin that he could not conceive what they could have done in a battle. "Wellington's Scottish Highlanders," Goethe replied, "were a different set of heroes, from all accounts." Eckermann replied: "I saw them in Brussels a year before the battle of Waterloo. They were men! All strong, nimble and free as if they had come straight from the hand of God. They carried their heads so freely and gaily and marched so lightly, swinging along with their bare knees, that you would have thought they had never heard of original sin or the primal curse." That does not look like the picture of a lazy or starving race. Yet these men were brought up in the Highlands, many of them on those very crofts that excited the Duke of Sutherland's appalled consternation; and a great proportion of them returned after the Napoleonic wars, to be evicted along with their kindred. The sheep-runs which replaced their homes were not so profitable as the Duke of Sutherland had foreseen; so that even economically the change did not justify itself. In the long run it has proved disastrous in every way. The glens from which the crofters were driven a century ago still lie waste. I have passed through them. Their soil is very like that of the Orkney Islands, and the Orkneys are now the most prosperous farming community in Scotland. A century ago they were probably as poor as the region that the Duke of Sutherland turned into a wilderness. The progress in the science of cultivation has since made them a happy and productive community, and it might quite well have done the same for the wide glens of Sutherlandshire.

It is difficult now to understand why the Duke of Sutherland, who seems to have been a kind and enlightened man, should have rooted out a whole people with such barbarity. It was mainly, I think, because at that time intelligent men's minds were possessed by a dream of general wealth for society, which would be realised by adhering to the latest economic principles, and by the natural and beneficent growth of Capitalism. One can begin to understand the strength of this Utopian passion if one reads Macaulay's extraordinary essay on Southey's *Colloquies*. Macaulay was writing at a time of great distress. But Southey's suggestion that the life of a country labourer might be more desirable than that of a factory worker put him into a blind rage. Southey had drawn a somewhat flattering picture of an English rustic cottage with its clipped box, roses, bee-hives and orchard, and had continued: "How is it that everything which is connected with manufactures presents such features of unqualified deformity? From the largest of Mammon's temples down to the poorest hovel in which his helotry are stalled, these edifices have all one character. Time will not mellow them; nature will neither clothe nor conceal them; and they will remain always as offensive to the eye as to the mind." Macaulay burst out: "Here is wisdom. Here are the principles on which nations are to be governed. Rose-bushes and poor-rates, rather than steam-engines and independence. Mortality and cottages with weather-stains, rather than health and long life with edifices which time cannot mellow. We are told, that our age has invented atrocities beyond the imagination of our fathers; that society has been brought into a state compared with which extermination would be a blessing; and all because the dwellings of the cotton-spinners are naked and rectangular. Mr. Southey has found out a way, he tells us, in which the effects of manufactures and agriculture may be compared. And what is this way? To stand on a hill, to look at a cottage and a factory and see which is the prettier."

Macaulay went on for a long time in this strain, never seeing Southey's point, which was that the rose-bushes, the clipped box and the bee-hives meant more than their surface prettiness, and the naked dwellings of the cotton-spinners more than their obvious ugliness: that, in short, they were expressions of two different ways of life, one in his opinion more desirable than the other. And if Macaulay could not see this, how was the Duke of Sutherland to do so, particularly as he was dealing with a people remote from him, whose cottages were very scantily furnished with rose-bushes, and quite without clipped box? The eyes of progressive people were fixed at that time on a different dream, and so what Southey said seemed wicked nonsense to them, as wicked as the complaints of the evicted Highlanders seemed to Mrs. Beecher Stowe.

Macaulay ended his essay with as good a description of this dream as one could find. "If we were to prophesy," he said, "that in the year 1930 a population of fifty millions, better fed, clad and housed than the English of our time, will cover these islands, that Sussex and Huntingdonshire will be wealthier than the wealthiest parts of the West Riding of Yorkshire now are, that cultivation, rich as that of a flower-garden, will be carried up to the very tops of Ben Nevis and Helvellyn, that machines constructed on principles yet undiscovered will be in every house, that there will be no highways but railroads, no travelling but by steam, that our debt, vast as it seems to us, will appear to our great-grandchildren a trifling encumbrance which might easily be paid off in a year or two, many people would think us insane." He did not prophesy this, he went on to say, though he might safely have risked most of his prognostications, except that cultivation rich as that of a flower-garden would be carried up to the very top of Ben Nevis; for by an ironical fatality a man who nursed the same dream as himself had put an end for a century to the cultivation of many humbler peaks in the Highlands, and even of the valleys lying between them. But this was the dream that caught up the Duke of Sutherland along with many other men of his time who had not such power to do harm; and compared with it the fate of a distant and supposedly ignorant peasantry did not matter. That dream came true in very much the form that Macaulay prophesied. Great Britain at present contains over forty millions of people better fed, clad and housed than the population of Macaulay's time; machines constructed on principles then undiscovered are in a great number of their houses; people travel by methods more comfortable and expeditious even than Macaulay foretold, and the national debt which troubled him so much would certainly seem small to them, for they have a far greater one of their own to shoulder. The dream has come true, indeed has far excelled the utmost hopes of Macaulay, except in the matter of Sussex and Huntingdonshire and Ben Nevis. Yet what sounded so fine as a dream is unsatisfactory as a reality, perhaps because a nation may lead a life which is not satisfying even though it has a number of machines in its houses, travels by steam or oil, and is able to shoulder a magnificent debt. But Macaulay could not understand that, and still less could the Duke of Sutherland; for they were the unconscious instruments of an economic change, and they regarded as self-evident the sacrifices which certain sections of the population had to suffer in order to bring that change about. They had no understanding of the Highland crofter who, though he lived more poorly than the cotton-spinner, lived also with more human satisfaction. They did not care very greatly what happened to the population if wealth could only be increased. I think this should be insisted upon, for it is this particular ideal of progress that has depopulated the Highlands and reduced them to the status of a backward region. They were robbed of their life by exactly the same process which built Glasgow. Anyone who wishes to get a true and impartial picture of this process should read Mr. Neil Gunn's fine novel about the clearances, *Butcher's Broom*.

The destruction of Highland life on a large scale began with the severities that followed Culloden. The second stage in it was the clearances. The third is still continuing, and its symbol may be found in the pictures of slaughtered animals that disfigure the walls of Highland hotels. Scott and Queen Victoria were probably the two people most responsible for this last disastrous phase. Scott sent the tourist wandering over the Highland hills, and Queen Victoria built Balmoral. The net result of these two innocent actions was to turn the Highlands into a huge game preserve covered with fences and dotted with notices making the pedestrian a trespasser. Consequently a great part of the Highland population now depend for their living on their obsequious skill in rendering the slaughter of wild creatures more easy or convenient to the foreign owners of the shooting lodges, and in performing whatever other menial services these people may require. The Highlanders' numbers have been thinned, their mode of life degraded, by a series of objective calamities. They have kept through all these changes their courtesy, their dignity, and one might almost say their freedom, for that seems to exist independently of any service, however menial, which they may render. But these qualities are bought at the expense of the disdainful resignation which a proud people feels in acknowledging defeat, a resignation so profound that it can treat its conqueror with magnanimity, while keeping him at his distance. Whether that is a good quality or a bad one I do not know, but it is in any case an extraordinary one.

It was through a perfectly waste area of the Highlands that I drove next day on my way to Ullapool on the West Coast. A soft rain had set in and it accompanied me for the whole breadth of Scotland. After the first stretch of pleasant green wooded country that lies inland from Beauly the landscape grew more and more wild. All that I could see of it was the little circle of visibility, a circle with a diameter of about half a mile, that travelled on with me. As the road mounted the rain thickened into low clouds—cold, clammy, and indeterminate shapes that seemed to rotate slowly in a circular plateau hemmed in by peaks which I could not see but only feel by a sixth sense. I stopped the car once or twice to get relief from the peculiarly lonely and foolish sound that it made in this amorphous solitude; and then a silence so oppressive set in that I felt that I could almost hear the rubbing of the clouds against the wet grass and rock and heather. It was as if a vast hand were clumsily pressing down this silence; the density of the clouds kneading everything together with a soft enclosing movement. Heavy drops lay on every blade of grass like a cold sweat, and yet the little circle of visibility remained, as though a pocket of light had slipped down here and were continuously bracing itself and making a fragile vault. In that circle blunt-looking rocks appeared and disappeared now and then, producing an effect as abrupt as if they were living things that had stepped out of the cloud and stepped back again. But except for them there was nothing but the black glistening road, the tangled heather, and the perpetual almost

inaudible drip-dripping of the bodiless rain, falling
slowly from just overhead.

After a long but busy imprisonment in this circle
(for the car was running quite well), I saw with relief
that I was going downwards; the clouds slowly settled
a little higher against the invisible hills; and soon I
was passing bright green larch woods, lodge gates
appeared, and one or two figures, apparently bent on
errands of their own, materialised on the road.
Presently, looking downwards, I found that the car
was running high above Loch Broom. The drip-drip
of the rain in the woods gave a peculiar secrecy to this
new landscape, and seemed to make even the clear
waters of the loch more immobile, so that I felt they
would lie there without a ripple until something unimaginable happened. The air was drenched in the
wet scent of larch and fir; the road wound up and
down through woods so bright that they seemed new-
made; and it was almost a shock when I caught sight
of the white walls and black roofs of Ullapool at a
sudden bend, for they seemed to have no relation to
the green watery world through which I was still passing. The town looked like a woodcut hung in a garden
bower. I found when I reached it that it was a very
pleasant little place.

It was only one o'clock when I arrived, but as there
seemed no prospect that the rain would stop I decided
to stay for the day. The hotel was full, mostly of
English people, and I should have had the sense to
change from my oily and mud-stained flannels before

I went into the dining-room. However, I was hungry and in my own country, and still so much under the influence of the scenes I had passed through that for quite a long time I could not understand the glares that greeted me from the surrounding tables. I found out later in the afternoon that a code of etiquette had been established in the hotel by the southern visitors, and that I had unwittingly violated it. The Scottish boarders, I discovered, had obsequiously adopted it, and no doubt I would have adopted it too had I stayed long enough; for once a tone is set in any place one requires almost a dash of moral perversity not to fall in with it. A part of the code in this particular hotel, I found out by the evening, was to meet in the drawing-room before dinner for sherry or cocktails; and this convention was so inviolable that even those among the Scottish contingent who were teetotallers piously attended the ceremony. By this time, having changed my clothes and proved myself amenable in other ways, I had been forgiven and even invited to take a hand at bridge. But one stout and gruff old gentleman with a public-school tie and a kilt was still not quite reconciled, and in a timid way, for I fancy he was quite kind-hearted, did his best to snub me.

I am always at a loss when I find myself among public-school boys, old or young, and one of the most disconcerting experiences I have ever had happened one Saturday at Twickenham, when I chanced to plunge right into a cloud of them in my wish to see a Rugby International between England and Wales.

The best way in which I can describe my sensations is that I felt myself in the centre of an overwhelming unanimity the terms of which I could account for by no conceivable exercise of my mind, a unanimity which found expression in saying at every moment exactly the right thing. I was immensely impressed, somewhat downcast, and quite astonished by this mechanical perfection of response, this unquestioning assurance that the game of life can be played only in one way, and that that way is known to everyone who has been to a public school. There were public-school girls there too, for one of them kept shouting "Go through him, Smith" to one of the English three-quarters whenever he was tackled by a Welshman; and this too, surprisingly enough, turned out to be the right thing to say. It is the ability to say such things as "Go through him, Smith," "Well played, sir," or "Ramsay MacDonald is a fine fellah" at the right moment that creates the tone I have been trying to give some idea of, and I have described my own inability to cope with it because I feel sure that that is shared by the majority of Highlanders, who have never been to public schools and do not know whether they are saying the right thing or not. "The gillie is so nice" was the most popular of these sentiments in the North; at least I heard it in all the Highland hotels I stopped at, uttered in every case by middle-aged Englishwomen. As a sentiment it was understandable enough, for the Highlanders are a polite people; but most of the rest of the conversations over the cocktails was quite incomprehensible to me, and when a remark was accepted as peculiarly right I honestly could not tell why.

This habit of the English upper middle-classes of immediately establishing a code of manners whenever a few of them are gathered together, and of requiring everybody else to subscribe to it, is very queer. A Scotsman, in spite of his angularity of character, will adapt himself to the customs of any foreign country he may be in, and try to fit himself into the picture out of a feeling of propriety. But there is a type of Englishman (and Englishwoman) who reacts in exactly the opposite way, and it is impossible to say whether he does it out of arrogance, or of uneasiness, or of a mixture of both, or of a mere mechanical response to habit. From the piety with which these sherry and cocktail ceremonies were observed one might have thought that behind them was a sacred idea, such as the greatness of the British Empire; but there seemed to be a faint tinge of anxiety in them too, as if something were threatened and these harmless drinks washed the invisible danger away. I became aware of an extraordinary watchfulness; it may have been merely that those English people assembled fortuitously in a strange hotel did not know each other's addresses and clubs. But there was also that nervously maintained unanimity; and one felt that if it were shattered something terrible, or at least extremely unedifying, would happen, something almost like an exposure of nakedness. I felt relieved when the cocktails were safely drunk and I could retire to my solitary table.

In the afternoon I went for a stroll through the soft rain. The streets lay empty in their wet whiteness. On the dripping pier a young Highlander with a waterproof apron tied round his kilt was waiting beside a motor-boat. The waters of the loch were quite smooth. I walked up and down the pier for some time until I found a run of wooden steps leading down to an underground gallery almost level with the sea. There, protected from the rain, I walked about for a long time, listening to the drip of the water from the planks overhead and the murmur of the tide as it sluggishly flowed round the rotting piles. Innumerable star-fish, living and dead, were glued to the glistening black baulks, and shoals of little fishes skimmed over them every now and then as heedlessly as if they belonged to a different world. The water dripped, filling the little gallery with tiny echoes that sounded like shivering glass. I do not know why, but soft rain in the Highlands makes them seem twice as remote, so that one cannot imagine they are within reach of anywhere. A boy and a young woman presently appeared with a collection of suit-cases and got into the motor-boat along with the young Highlander. The engine started and in a few minutes they had all been swallowed up in the mist.

I went to bed early to escape a threatened hand at bridge. When I tried to start the car next morning I could make nothing of it. A young mechanic belonging to the hotel tinkered gravely with the plugs for a while. The garage attendants in the Lowlands had always shown a sympathetic, humorous interest in my conveyance; but this young Highlander treated it with as much respectful concern as if it had been a Rolls-Royce, and did not give the faintest sign that he saw its comic possibilities. He was not really any kinder than the Lowland mechanics had been, but he showed a different consideration for my feelings, or rather for what I might conceivably have felt; for the garage happened to be filled with a dozen cars, all of which looked splendid beside mine, and it would have been easy for any hard-pressed garage hand to regard my engine troubles with impatience. But nothing of the kind happened, and I felt again that I was in a different country.

Up to Ullapool I had been driving over good and moderately level roads. From now on I was to find myself climbing up and down mountain sides over surfaces little better than a cart-track. There must have been something wrong with the plugs, as the young mechanic had said; at any rate I noticed that on the first gradient the car seemed to be complaining more than usual. Then I came to a long, rough, steep rise. I got up full speed and covered a little stretch of it in third gear, then switched to second, and finally to first. The car went more and more slowly, seemed to waver for a moment, and stopped. I was only two-thirds up the hill, hanging precariously at what seemed to me an angle of forty-five degrees. I started the

engine again, speeded it up until it roared, slipped
the clutch into first gear, jerked the car up a few yards,
and then rested it. In this way, by a series of jerks, I
got the car up to the top, hoping that this was the
worst hill I would have to climb. About a dozen
powerful easy-moving cars from the hotel passed me
while I was in the middle of this grass-hopper act. My
hopes that I had survived the worst, however, were
soon dashed; for I presently found myself jerking up a
still worse mountain. If I had known more about the
car I might have saved myself a great deal of distress
for the next few days, for I am certain that there must
have been something wrong with the plugs. As it was
I was doomed to jerk myself up all the hill roads of
the western and northern Highlands from Ullapool to
Tongue, and sweat and curse among the strangest and
most magnificent scenery. At one point in this curious
journey I jerked off without knowing it a suit-case
containing all my clothes; the engine was making too
much noise for anything else to be heard. But I shall
come to that later; and this is all I intend to say about
my troubles with the car. They filled my mind in the
most curious way, nevertheless, creating a sort of little
private hell from which I looked out like Dives on to
the heavenly beauty of the north-western Highland
mountains.

The thing which impresses one most about the wild
scenery in this part of the Highlands is its strangeness.
Geologists give the explanation that the mountains
here consist of two formations which have piled up in

confusion, so that the summits belonging to one of
them sometimes burst through the surface of the other.
One's actual impression of these peaks is that they do
not belong to the world we know at all, but to a much
older one; I had this feeling before I knew the
geological explanation of it. The ordinary sensations
which mountains arouse do not fit these extraordinary
rock shapes; and yet they are not terrifying in any way,
but merely strange beyond the power of the mind to
fathom. Part of their strangeness may, no doubt, be
explained by the abruptness with which they start up
out of places which seem to have no connection with
them. The movement of wild mountain scenery is
generally a tossing movement as of waves. On the
surface the scenery of Western Sutherlandshire has this
tossing movement, but the summits of which I have
been speaking rise out of these billows like rocks out
of a sea and seem to have a different consistency and
to belong to a different order. They are bold and
regular and yet unexpected in their shape, as if they
were the result of a wild kind of geometry. One sees
huge cones with their tops smoothly sliced off to form
a circular plateau, gigantic pyramids, and even shapes
that seem top-heavy, so that one cannot understand on
what principle they remain upright. Round about
these isolated peaks rolls in large even swells a sea of
lower mountains, from whose shapes one can perceive
that they have been moulded by time, for they have its
rise and fall and its continuity of rhythm. But these
older cones and pyramids seem to have no connection

with time at all; they are unearthly not in any vague but in a quite solid sense, like blocks of an unknown world scattered blindly over a familiar one. The thoughts they evoke are neither heavenly nor terrifying, but have a sort of objective strangeness and give one the same feeling one might have if one could have a glimpse of an eternal world, such as the world of mathematics, which had no relation to our human feelings, but was composed of certain shapes which existed in complete changeless autonomy.

Having jerked myself up several hills I landed at last at Kylesku Ferry, where I found I had to wait three hours for the tide. By this time the sun had come out again and the sea in the little inland loch was bright blue against the purplish-grey mountains. I found that I had done six miles an hour and that my right arm was sore with changing gears and pulling the brake. When I arrived I found a family of Australians, a father and two daughters, who had been at the hotel in Ullapool, and they told me that they too had been quite overawed by the cocktail ceremony, so that they had not dared to open their mouths. They told me also that they found it much easier to talk to people in Scotland than in England. They had begun their holiday in London, but during the fortnight they had stayed in a hotel there they had not spoken to a single human being except for the hotel servants. We talked of this and of the Highland deer forests, one of which took up all the hills and valleys we were looking at. With the incoming tide jelly-fishes in great numbers began to float past the little point where we sat. Except for two or three huts beside the ferry there was not a human habitation in sight. Nor in all the expanse of tree-less deer forest could I see a single movement to betray the presence of a living creature.

North from Kylesku I escaped the steep hills for a time, and the landscape in general became lower and more ordinary. As I reached the sea the car wound in and out among rocky gorges for a time. Then I suddenly found myself looking down on a bay filled with small rocky islets, and far beyond them, on the horizon, the long misty outline of Lewis. I stopped for a while to enjoy the unexpectedness of the sight, for these little islets had the strangeness which I had felt in the high geometrical peaks, and seemed to belong to the same world, reproducing it on a small scale. Whether I was right in thinking this, I do not know; it is difficult to tell which world one is in as one passes through these landscapes, especially if, like myself, one has little or no knowledge of geology. Or that little drove of islands—they seemed to be nothing but rock, and yet an odd tree or two grew from them—may have belonged to a private world of their own. All I know is that they seemed as remote from human life as the huge peaks, and as impervious to all the sentimental associations which nature usually evokes in one's mind. There were one or two cottages on the shore overlooking this tiny archipelago, and smoke was rising from their chimneys in the calm evening air, a sight which for a reason I know of always awakens in me a

214

host of sentimental memories; but here it awakened none at all; the impression of strangeness given by the little islands was too strong.

One could imagine oneself being so deeply influenced by this scenery, if one lived close to it for a long time, that one's most simple feelings about human life would be changed. I think something of this kind must have happened in the little town of Scourie, to which I presently came. In its very formation it seems to be in two minds, like the landscape around it. The houses that make it up are planted at the most abrupt intervals; one finds two or three quite close together, then a few fields, another house, fields again, a hotel on a little rise, a row of houses beyond it that have the air of belonging to a suburban avenue, a farm to one side, and at a good distance from all these, as if it existed in itself, a pier and harbour at the head of a neat and narrow little firth. Not very far from the pier, but away from the village, is a beautiful old house such as one would expect to find in the more cultivated parts of the Borders, and immediately behind it rises a wild hill of bare rippling rock. Beyond the hotel, at a little distance, rises another hill of the same rippling black rock, at whose foot lies a loch, black as ink, and by its look very deep. The village shop adjoins the hotel, and a group of well-set-up young men were standing talking and laughing in front of it when I arrived. It was Saturday evening.

The hotel was comfortably filled with English anglers, a peaceful set of men whose dreamy voices

filled the dining-room with dim and watery reminiscences, in which one could hear the lapping of
lake water and the day-long purling of streams. They
drank a great deal of beer in a quiet hypnotic way,
and their voices never rose and never stopped, but
babbled on in the most tranquil way imaginable, so
that one soon began to feel sleepy. I went for a walk
along a cart-track leading up one of the hills, from
which I could look down into the black loch. The
ripples running under the surface of the hill looked
exactly like those that break the smoothness of a big
wave. The light was quite clear, though it was ten
o'clock, and I had definitely for the first time the feeling of being in the real north. I turned back again,
for the blackness of the loch was a little frightening,
wandered past one or two houses, crossed a foot-bridge
over a little stream lined with tall irises, passed
through a green field, and found myself at the pier,
where a young man and a young woman were wash-
ing nets. The youths who had been standing outside
the shop were dispersing in groups along the roads,
and I returned to the hotel and to my bed.

I started next morning quite early, for I had made
up my mind to be at Scrabster next day in time to
catch the boat to Orkney; and though the distance was
not great, I knew the limitations of the car and did
not know what mountains might still lie in front of
me. For most of the forenoon I found to my surprise
that the going was not very difficult; cool, misty
weather had set in, and the engine did not get so hot

as usual; the road, having mounted steadily for a while, wound in and out among little broken hills among which were scattered a confusion of small lochs, all black and somewhat sinister-looking; there was no sign of a dwelling, nor of life of any kind, during all this stretch. Presently the sun came out again, showing that I was at the top of an immense long glen sweeping down towards what looked like level land. Five or six crofters' dwellings with no sign of movement about them (for it was Sunday) lay scattered on the vast slopes: and far away in front I thought I could see a faint quivering in the air, which must have been the sea. I passed a house beside the road with its doors and windows shut, and a little distance from it a few cattle in a field, the first of these animals that I have seen since leaving Dunkeld. I let the car roll of itself down the long descent, giving it a needed rest, and at the foot, in a desolation of sand-dunes, perceived a large, white and polished hotel a little distance away from the road. It seemed to have no right to be there; but I surmised the close neighbourhood of a trout loch, and held on for Durness, knowing that it could not be far away. Presently I saw it huddled grey under a great cloud that had come up, a little rickle of houses, half of them uninhabited, half in ruins, all clean as if they had been sand-polished. I went into a tea-room and lunched on cold ham and lemonade.

As I left Durness I saw a round hill rising out of the sea far away to the north-east, whose shape seemed somehow familiar to me. It was, I realised, the hill of Hoy in Orkney, which I had never seen before from this angle; and it seemed strange to me that for the people of Durness that mound must be a constant shape on the horizon, as well known to them as the inside of their houses; and I thought that all our lives are bounded by a similar horizon, which is at once familiar to us and beyond our knowledge, and that it is against this indistinct barrier that our imaginings pile themselves up, building for all of us a fabulous world. I tried to think of Hoy as an outline on the horizon which never came nearer; and because I knew the Orkneys, having lived in them during my childhood, I had a sense stronger than ever before of the double aspect of everything, and realised that if it had been possible for me to live in two places at once, in Durness, say, and my father's farm in Orkney, my life there would have seemed to one part of me merely a dream in the shadow of that round hill rising from the sea. This thought disturbed me, for it seemed to point to a sort of ultimate isolation of every human being, an isolation produced by the mere workings of time and space, which therefore no ideal state or Utopia could ever reform away. I told myself that this was a figment of my imagination, but knew it was not as I looked at that hill which I seemed to know by two faculties at once, which I had so much wished to see, but had never expected to see like this. And I reflected that all the strange scenery which I had gazed at during my two-days' journey had just as little rela-

tion to it as it was known by the few people who
lived among it, as that round hill in the sea to
Orkney.

Somewhat east of Durness the long and narrow
Loch Eriboll makes a deep indentation into the land,
and I had now for several hours to coast round it on
scarred roads. At the head of the loch are two great
mountain peaks, less geometrically regular than the
ones I had passed further south, but with the same
solitary prominence, and as I drove slowly over the
uneven stony surface I saw a huge cloud gathering over
them. Presently a thick veil of rain came sweeping
towards me over the intervening country. The sun was
shining further to the west, and its rays cut a glitter-
ing swathe through the edge of the advancing rain,
which at its centre was a black wall that grew taller
and taller as it advanced, till it shut out the sky. I
stopped the car, put up the hood, and lit a cigarette.
Every living thing seemed to be waiting for that wave
to sweep over it: the long grasses along the road were
quite motionless; then I saw them trembling and
waving beneath the soft gust of air that the wall of
rain drove before it, and a moment afterwards a few
drops pattered down: then a whole cataract descended
on the roof of the car. The grasses, driven down flat,
rebounded madly as if fighting for their life; shoots of
light erratically pierced through the tumult of flying
water from the sun still shining brightly somewhere
behind the cloud; in a little while it shone in full
force, though the fringes of the shower were still

trailing past the hills. Then in a few minutes the air was quite hot and still again, and as I put up the hood a grey cloud of horse-flies descended on me. I hastily started the car to get rid of them, but I was to see more of them later on. I now had a clear view of the wild rocky outline of the east coast of Loch Eriboll, a tossing confusion of black bluffs, which gave an impression of panic flight as they swept outwards towards the open sea. It was the wildest, though not the strangest, scenery I had come to in the Highlands until now, and in that Sunday stillness, on the deserted road, it was a little frightening.

I was now approaching nearer and nearer to the two great peaks that guarded the head of the loch, and was presently running along a level road to the opposite side, through a marsh covered with tall grasses. Presently I came to a steep and long hill, up which I proceeded to jerk myself in the usual way. Here the horse-flies appeared again; they came in great numbers and floated past between me and the windscreen like a thin dangling moth-eaten veil. As soon as the car dropped to first gear they settled all over it and me. Both my hands were fully occupied in the complicated process of jerking the car up-hill. I went on as composedly as possible; but when I felt the horrible creatures crawling over my lips I became flustered, and just on the very top edge of the hill I pushed down the brake too hard and the car stopped. I flailed my arms through the air for a while and pushed the starter with my foot; but the engine would not start, so I got out and tinkered with the plugs in a cloud of horse-flies, which I tried to disperse by smoking one cigarette after another. At last a car appeared coming in the opposite direction, and the driver got down, un-screwed the plugs, did something or other to them, and started the car. I shall always feel grateful to him, whoever he was. In a little while I had jerked myself up to the top of the hill, where as if by general agree-ment the horse-flies turned back. It was on this hill that I must have tumbled off my suitcase, though I did not realise it until two hours later, when I reached Tongue. But by that time I was so terrified of the hills and the horse-flies that I would not have returned for a hundred pounds. So I reported the loss to the local constable, and duly received the suit-case, and all that was in it, quite unharmed, a fortnight later in Orkney.

But between Loch Eriboll and Tongue I had to pass through several more of these hot and breathless moun-tain valleys filled with horse-flies. The heat and the silence would have made these places sinister in any case, but the horse-flies intensified this impression immeasurably, perhaps because they were the same colour as the heather and looked like a dusty veil risen from it and armed with malignant power, an animate part of the landscape. In spite of the recent showers the air in these hollows had an arid burnt taste; and the dry, soft, almost gentle onset of these loathsome winged creatures was besides horribly deliberate. They seemed to gauge the speed of the car, know that when the road grew steep both my hands would be fully occupied, and calmly take advantage of the situation. To find these quite deserted valleys covered with horse-flies was also so strange that it gave me a superstitious feeling: for what blood could they find to suck in such places, all dead as the valley of bones?

I had tea at Tongue and lingered over it somewhat fearfully. But for the rest of my way I was not troubled with a single horse-fly. The road, too, was comparatively level, for the hills had receded. I passed a bay of beautiful white sand, and watched the Orkney Islands draw nearer in the bright evening light. After I had passed the little village of Bettyhill, where the road was filled with a black-coated crowd going to evening service, I overtook for the first time in my journey a car which was more down at heels than my own, driven somewhat apprehensively by two young men who looked like farm labourers. When I got to Melvich, a little village on the Pentland Firth, I decided to stop for the night, for it was by then after eight o'clock. As I was putting up my car at the garage the two young men appeared at it on foot: their car had broken down. Their apprehensions had been justified.

The evening I spent at Melvich was the pleasantest of all my journey. The hotel was unexpectedly comfortable and well-run, and the walls were quite without the usual bleeding array of pictured carcases. I had actually dreamt of a frieze of such walls one night in a hotel unusually well furnished with them; so that

the relief with which I saw the clean walls of the
Melvich Hotel, though it may seem excessive, was
quite understandable to myself. I arrived long after
dinner was over, but the lady who ran the place provided me with a better meal—cold chicken and
dessert—than I had had in any of the other hotels.
As I had only a drive of a dozen miles over a fairly
level and good road next day, and this evening
solemnised the end of my jerks, I decided to allow
myself a bottle of wine, and was provided with a very
good one. When I finished my dinner about half-past
nine the light was still perfectly clear, so I went for a
walk past the straggling houses of the little village
until I came to the shore. The outlines of the Orkney
hills were still distinct, and the evening had that perfect tranquillity which I have always associated for
some reason with Sunday evenings, when the very
quality of the light seems different. I wandered about
the shore for some time in this strangely distinct and
yet dream-like clarity. I stayed there until about
eleven o'clock; watched the shadows of the cliffs
motionlessly reflected in the sea, the Orkney hills
blown like bubbles against the colourless sky, the
horse and cattle near-by cropping the grass—the tear-
ing of their teeth and the pounding of their hooves
sounding strangely loud in that stillness and at that
hour—and a few silent couples scattered here and there
over the soft turf along the cliff-tops. When I turned
in the outline of everything had become softer, but
was still perfectly clear, and the windows of the houses

gleamed brightly, appearing still to hold the fullness
of the light after it had faded from the walls. At
twelve o'clock as I was going to bed I looked out
through the window of my room and saw some horses
in a field still moving about restlessly in the light,
and occasionally pawing the ground with their hooves.
The outline of the Orkneys had almost faded away,
and was like a dark breath on the horizon.

During all my way from Edinburgh my mind had
been slightly but pleasantly troubled in the evening,
but especially at bedtime, by a sort of illusion, partly
optical and partly temporal, which must be known to
everyone who covers a good stretch of country in an
open car. The place I started from in the morning
seemed suddenly to have dropped an immeasurable
distance behind and to be almost in a different world.
All the impressions of the day, all the landscapes that
had followed so fast on one another, seemed to have
built up an impregnable barrier between me and the
place where that morning I had eaten a quite ordinary
breakfast, and to have clothed it in the atmosphere of
landscapes seen many years before. Yet at the same
time I could see myself starting the car from that very
place ten hours ago; indeed, I could almost feel it, as
if my muscles remembered. This double sensation of
time was confusing and yet pleasant, and evoked in
my imagination an unusually vivid sense of the
simultaneity of the many lives and towns and landscapes scattered over the world, the countless human
and animal and material things co-existing there con-

temporaneously in a thousand forms, unaware of the life beyond their horizons, and yet following the same laws as it. From this indistinct and yet vivid image I tried to extract a picture of Scotland as an entity, but I did not succeed: I could envisage the world in these terms, though I had seen very little of it; I could see people everywhere, in the plains of China, the jungles of India, the villages of England, the snows of Greenland, following out the law of their being and of being itself, in isolation from the rest of their fellow-men and in inner harmony with them; but I could not think of any modification of the law of being that fitted Scotland and Scotland alone, any Scottish way of life that would embrace all the ways of life that I had observed from the time I had left Edinburgh for the Borders, the Borders for Glasgow, and Glasgow for the Highlands. I had to admit to myself that I had seen a great number of things, but no thing, and to fall back on the conclusion that nationality is real and yet indefinable, and that it can be grasped at most in history, which means that it cannot really be grasped at all, since history is continuous and unbreak-able, extending in its written state behind us and in its unwritten state before us, and can never be seized in its entirety until there is nobody to seize it. I tried to cast my mind back into Scottish history, and since in history every event seems determined by other events, so that nothing could have happened other than it happened, I saw that Scotland must have had the only history that it could have had, and the one species of nationality that suited it, and that present-day Scotland, in spite of the dissatisfaction that it awakens in all Scotsmen who stop to think of it, is just as much an essential expression of Scottish history as the Scotland of Robert Bruce, or James IV, or John Knox, or the Jacobite and rationalist eighteenth century. A nation has a development; the things that happen to it possess a logic in which is concentrated what we call its national spirit; and whether we like it or not, the Scotland we know, the Scotland of the present day, must be the inevitable result of the Scottish spirit, and its sole extant expression.

This deterministic conclusion discouraged me when I came to it, and I went over in my mind what Scottish history I could remember, hoping to find some faint sign that Scotland's annals need not have been so calamitous as they were, and need not have led to the end of Scotland as a nation. I thought of the declaration of independence signed at Arbroath Abbey on April 6th, 1320: "As long as a hundred of us remain alive, we will never submit to the domination of the English: for we fight not for glory, nor riches, nor honour, but for liberty alone, which no good man giveth up save with life itself." I thought of Barbour's fine lines on freedom. But I reflected that Wallace had been betrayed, that David I had sold his country; I saw the first four Jameses thwarted on every side, Mary Stuart sold to the English, Charles I sold to the English, and Scotland itself sold to the English. I remembered Culloden and the Highland clans delivered helpless to Cumberland because of the intrigues and counter-intrigues of their chieftains and a few Lowland Scots; I thought of the present feud between Glasgow and Edinburgh, the still continuing antipathy between the Highlands and the Lowlands; and it seemed to me that the final betrayal of Scotland which made it no longer a nation was merely the inevitable result, the logical last phase, of the intestine dissensions which had all through its history continued to rend it. I thought of the Covenanters at Bothwell Brig fighting one another and flying from their enemy; and that seemed to me a symbol of Scottish history and of the Scottish spirit, which even now is kinder to strangers than to those who were nursed in it. And there came into my mind a sight that I had seen as I stood on the banks of an Austrian mountain stream on a very hot summer day many years before. The stream was running very fast, and in the middle I made out two bright green snakes struggling in a death battle; I watched them for a few moments; then they were both swept, still fighting, over a cataract. The comparison was too swift and dramatic, I told myself, for the stubborn anger that burns through Scottish history; but nevertheless it would have been as impossible to put a stop to that at any of the disastrous turns of Scottish history. Perhaps with time this spirit of exaggerated individualism will no longer be able to work the harm to Scotland that it has worked in the past. But that time is far away yet, for even the Scottish Nationalist Party, which was formed to bring about national unity, has already been weakened by dissensions within itself.

When we experience the shock of encountering a foreign people it does not often come into our minds that these people we meet are the result of a long process of history. About one's own people one hardly ever remembers it unless one thinks naturally in historical terms. In France, which has a particularly strong and definite tradition, this feeling comes easily into one's mind; and I have felt it very clearly, too, in parts of Southern England which have not been overlaid by industrial civilisation. In such places, with their old farms going back to the sixteenth or the fourteenth century, one has a sense of a civilisation very firmly rooted, and can understand why England is a place where people live, even now, under the most difficult and novel conditions, in peace with one another: they have had to do it for centuries, and the knack is in their blood. England had learned this art when Scotland was still in a lawless condition; and the difference between present-day Scottish and English life can be explained, it seems to me, by that historical fact.

The reason for the lawlessness of Scottish history has always appeared to me to be mainly a geographical one; I do not think this has been insisted upon as it should be. The south of England, the heart of English civilisation, was easy to reach from the capital at a time when communication was generally difficult and the reign of law only beginning. Except for a small area near its centre, most of Scotland was at the same crucial period almost inaccessible. The Stewart kings, a brilliant and capable line, equal in capacity to any dynasty that has sat on the English throne, tried to unite the country into a whole, and during a few years in the reign of James IV seemed to have almost succeeded. But that phase did not last, and could not have lasted even if the battle of Flodden had never been fought. The hills were too high, communications inadequate, and disaffection too easy.

It is claimed nowadays, however, that long before and for some time after this period there existed a highly developed Celtic civilisation both in the Highlands and the Lowlands. I do not know whether this was actually the case; the historical evidence for it seems somewhat inadequate: but if it was the case, then that civilisation was evidently without the power to coalesce into a unity; not a thing which one could call a nation, but merely a congeries of local septs; and in considering it we return to only another reason why the unstable equilibrium which we call Scotland should have dissolved under the flood of English gold that swept it into the Union. Almost all Scotland was Celtic at the time of the Stewarts, we are told, and Gaelic was spoken in the Lowlands two hundred years ago. I do not hold with this view of Scottish history; but even if one were to admit it, and allow that the people were Celtic, they have abundantly shown through many centuries a striking incapacity to unite and to prevail. There are obvious reasons for this, if one accepts the above hypothesis. The Highland clans have a long tradition of mutual jealousy which still persists to-day in a peaceful form, and the antipathy between the Stewarts and the Campbells is a part of history. But that is merely an example of a hundred others, round which romantic legend has grown up. It is not surprising, considering all this, that the refrain of the old Celtic song which impressed Matthew Arnold so much should have run: "They went out to battle, but they were always defeated"; and one cannot help concluding that they were defeated for the same reason that the Covenanters were defeated at Bothwell Brig: that is, because they fought among themselves. I am not inclined to question the age or the genuineness of the Celtic civilisation, for the Highlanders have all the marks of a highly civilised people. But in Scotland that civilisation has always been disunited for one thing, and for another has left behind it an astonishingly meagre record of its existence. A little poetry, a number of lovely songs, some beautiful pipe music, hardly any sculpture or architecture, no painting, no philosophy, no science, and no sign of that conceptual intelligence which welds together and creates great and complex communities and makes possible the major achievements of art and science. If we accept the old theory that the Celtic population of Scotland has for a long time been confined to the Highlands, all this is easily explained by geography; for civilisation in its beginnings has always depended to a great degree on rich agricultural soil, easy communication, and trade; and these things for many centuries could not be had in the Highlands. But if we accept the theory that all Scotland was Celtic until a few hundred years ago, then there is no choice but to conclude that there was something in the Celtic civilisation which prevented it from developing as others have done, and kept it from achieving nationality or even from having the burden of nationality imposed permanently upon it.

Thus far I have been merely trying from an inadequate knowledge of Scottish history (and all Scottish history is inadequate and confusing; it has still to be written) to show why Scotland's existence as a nation was always unstable and incomplete, and why it finally dissolved. The reasons for this were partly geographical and partly racial, if the Celtic legend is to be given the credence that it is more and more acquiring. At present geography presents no obstacle to the union of Scotland: that problem has long since been solved. The Celtic civilisation, too, has fallen to pieces; the clans exist no longer except as names; even the Gaelic language is disappearing, and if its decline continues will have died in another hundred years. These various obstacles then—geographical inaccessibility, local culture, separate language—have almost vanished, and there seems to be no palpable hindrance to the union of Scotland as a nation. If there was a really strong demand for such a union, England could not withhold it, nor probably attempt to do so. The real obstacle to the making of a nation out of Scotland lies now in the character of the people, which is a result of their history, as their history was in a large measure of the things of which I have been speaking, geographical and racial. And that obstacle, being the product of several centuries of life, is a serious one; it is, in fact, Scotland.

It is these things that make the National Party of Scotland so unconvincing. One can see that self-government for Scotland is a desirable ideal, but like all Utopian ideals it takes no account of history, past or present; indeed, it takes less account of present than of past history. That being the case, where is the force that will drive the people of Scotland to proclaim themselves a nation? In the heads of a few people, mainly middle-class, with an admixture of the intelligentsia, who see that Scotland a nation is a desirable aim. But meanwhile the people themselves, like the people of every industrial country of Europe, are being driven by the logic of necessity to a quite different end, the most convenient term for which is Socialism. Who in such circumstances can take Scottish Nationalism seriously, or even wish that it should enjoy a brief triumph, when processes so much more serious and profound are at work in the whole of society? I have tried to approach the Scottish Nationalist movement as sympathetically as possible; I saw in my journey through Scotland the justification for it; I still see that its object is admirable. But there are numberless movements that are justified in themselves

and whose objects are admirable, and only one or two
in any age which can prevail, because they come out
of the deeper life that creates history. I think that in
a Douglasite or Socialist Britain Scotland would be
given liberty to govern itself; but I cannot think of
its achieving nationality in any other way; and a Parliament in Edinburgh made up of the Scottish members
at present sitting in Westminster is not an ideal which
can inspire a deep passion. Yet this is the object of
the National Party of Scotland as it is presently con-
stituted. At one time there were in it men who thought
they saw an opportunity in Nationalism of applying
the Douglas Scheme to Scotland, or even of making it
a Socialist state; but now the party has become safe
in its attempt to attract people of every opinion,
Liberal, Conservative and Socialist. That it should
throw out its Douglasites and Socialists was probably inevitable, and that they could have achieved their
aims through it was certainly impossible: changes in
society are not brought about by such clever notions.
The impulse of Scottish Nationalism at its best comes
from a quite sincere conviction that the course of Scottish history urgently needs to be changed; but it is
probable that the change can come only from outside,
from a change in the structure of civilised society in
general, by means of which all nations will be given
a new start and all peoples taken into a new federation. A hundred years of Socialism would do more
to restore Scotland to health and weld it into a real
nation than a thousand years—if that were conceivable

—of Nationalist government such as that to which the National Party of Scotland looks forward; for even if the country were governed by Scotsmen, the economic conflicts within it could still generate the same intestine hatreds as they do now, and would still deserve to do so.

Looking, then, at Scotland as impartially as I could, in the little room of the hotel on that last evening of my run, I seemed to see that it was ripe for two things: to become a nation, and to become a Socialist community; but I could not see it becoming the one without becoming the other. I thought of derelict Glasgow and the waste glens of Sutherland, and I saw that these could not be brought to life except by some general effort, whether national or communal or both. The Socialist movement in Scotland is still strong, in spite of the countless discouragements it has suffered; it is strong because it has behind it the drive of economic and historical reality. The National Party has nothing behind it but a desire and nothing before it but an ideal; and it is numerically so weak as to be negligible. These are facts that no amount of publicity and no degree of romanticising of realities can alter. If Scotland is changed, it will be changed by Socialists and Douglasites. And it is necessary that it should be changed by them. Scotland needs a hundred years of Douglasism to sweat out of it the individualism which destroyed it as a nation and has brought it where it is.

Next morning my car refused to start, and the young garage attendant spent a long time over the plugs, concern in his looks. At last he got the engine to go, and as there were only inclines, nothing that could be called hills, between me and Thurso, I started with an easy mind. But on the first slight rise the car began to flag, was presently down in its familiar first gear again, and would not budge except by roaring jerks which made an indecent din in the quiet country-side. A car coming in the opposite direction slowed down and an elderly colonel-like gentleman craned his neck out of it, looked at me in amazed disgust, gave a loud snort, and drove on. Presently a large lorry drew up behind me, and the young garage attendant got out saying that this would not do at all. I stopped the engine and he went over the plugs again, found that one was dead, fished another out of the tool-box, cleaned it, and screwed it in. After that the car took several long hills on third gear without complaint, and brought me into Thurso in style. The garage attendant kept a half-mile behind me all the way, in case I should have another break-down, I fancy: one of countless instances of Highland kindness. I met him in the streets of Thurso and thanked him and said good-bye before buying a pair of flannel trousers to keep me going until my clothes followed me.

A rain-cloud met me in the Pentland Firth as I neared Orkney; but the sea, for that treacherous and chancy stretch of water, was comparatively smooth. I watched it bubbling in smooth, glassy whirlpools round which the little "St. Ola" edged skilfully; great carbuncles of coiling water breaking the rippled sur face. It was the same boat that I had known thirty years before, when I went to school in Orkney, and I have been told that the captain very rarely takes the same route over this little stretch of water: the carbuncles shift continually, breaking out now here and now there. The weather is very rarely too rough for him to set out across this web of waters into which are braided the North Sea from one side and the Atlantic from the other; for many years he has crossed it twice a day in this absurd little tub of a boat, which jumps about like a cork, a bobbing trap for bad sailors.

My wife and my little boy were waiting for me at Scapa, and we set off for the house that we had taken for the summer. There we spent three months doing far less work than we had intended to do, meeting old friends and making new ones, and attempting a great many things that were quite idle and will not come into this book.

The Orkney Islands are such an interesting little community that they deserve a longer description than I have given to the places I stopped at in the Highlands; also I know them much better, having been brought up in them, and can speak of them with more confidence. They are far less spectacular than the Western Highlands, and the tourist in search of the immediately picturesque will find little to repay him in them. He will find no attempt, either, to entertain him; and I have heard of holiday-makers hopefully going to Orkney and after two days of appalled disillusion taking the boat back to Aberdeen or Leith,

and proceeding straight to Dunoon or Blackpool. He
will find a group of little islands, some quite flat, some
hilly, all of them almost treeless, and all remarkably
well and efficiently cultivated. He will also find a
population of small farmers and crofters, naturally
gentle and courteous in manners, but independent too,
and almost all of them moderately prosperous. If he
goes there in the middle of June, the long light, which
never fades at that time of the year, but ebbs and ebbs
until, before one can tell how, morning is there again,
will charm and tease him; he will lose his sleep for a
few nights and be discontented during the day, and
feel that he is not quite in the real world. If he has
an eye for such things, he will be delighted by the
spectacle of the quickly changing skies and the clear-
ness and brightness of all the colours. But he will not
come to know much about the place unless he lives
there for quite a long time, habituating himself to the
rhythm of the life, and training himself to be pleased
with bareness and simplicity in all things. Orkney is
full of fine scenery, but that has to be looked for, and
of historical interest, but that requires acquaintance
with a kind of history on which even experts are uncertain: the kind of history which is popularly called
prehistory. These islands are rich, for instance, in Pict
houses and underground chambers: standing in some
places one can see a score of these little hummocks
breaking the horizon-line. There are also brochs,
those curious circular keeps which still puzzle the most
skilful archæologists: a very impressive one was being

excavated last summer when I was there. In addition there are various remains of the Viking occupation of Orkney, the golden period of Orkney history, when Kirkwall was the capital of the Norse western empire. There is also a fine megalithic (or Druid, as it used to be called) ring, and an ancient burial-chamber estimated to be something like four thousand years old, on whose walls can still be seen the runes of a band of Vikings who broke into it, leaving news that they were on their way to Jerusalem. There are innumerable signs, in other words, that these islands have been richly populated for several thousands of years, and that one civilisation has followed another on them. Anyone who stays for very long in Orkney is consequently bound to turn into an amateur archæologist unless he has something more pressing to do. All these things, the bareness of the landscape with its strong colours, the vivid evidences of a past but strange life, the endlessly seductive contours of all these islands spread out in the sea (there are hills from which one can see them all at the same time) give Orkney a deep fascination for those who know it. But a tourist looking for scenery in the grand style, or for entertainment in any style, would find nothing of note in it, nothing but bare low hills and ordinary farmsteadings, and would probably be bored in a few days.

I do not intend to write about the scenery or the history of Orkney, however, but of its way of life. It is an agricultural community. The great majority of its farms are small and of a size that can be easily cultivated by the farmer and his family, without hiring outside labour. There are some large farms such as one finds in the south of Scotland and in England; but they are too few to affect the character of Orkney life, which is determined by these small, easily worked farms. Most of these farms are owned by their occupiers. In spite of their size, they are run on the most scientific modern lines; and this fact must be put to the credit of the Orkney people, who are unusually intelligent and adaptable; similar crofts in the western Highlands and the Hebrides, for instance, are still cultivated as they were in past ages. At the same time the life of the people on these farms is, in its main lines, what it was a hundred years ago. The farming community was poor then and it is prosperous now; that is almost the sole difference. A great number of the farmers have cars or motor-bicycles to go about on, it is true, and when the County Cattle Show, the great event of the year, takes place, there are aeroplanes to bring people from the distant islands to Kirkwall, the chief town. But these modern devices carry them to traditional events, to cattle-shows, markets, country dances and feasts such as their grandfathers and great-grandfathers attended. If one visits a farm-house one might be in an Orkney kitchen fifty years ago, except for the fact that food and drink are more plentiful. On these farms the people work steadily but easily enough; the life is not one of drudgery. The farmers go to bed late and get up late; one can drop into houses between ten and eleven at night and find the family sitting round the fire or playing games; and the cows are milked late so that one need not get up early in the morning to attend to them.

I spoke to a farmer about the economic depression, and asked him how it affected him. He admitted in a detached way that he was beginning to feel it, but that in any case he and his neighbours could carry on, even if it got worse, for they depended in the last resort on their farms. There is nobody at all in Orkney, I should say, who is enormously rich; there is hardly a trace of the widespread poverty that one finds both in the big towns and in the country-side of middle and southern Scotland. The prosperity of Orkney is due mostly to science. I paid a visit to two farms that my father had worked one after the other. In his time it had been a hard job to wring a living from them and pay the rent; now they are very pleasant, easily worked and profitable places. The same thing has happened all over Orkney, not only in the mainland, but in the smallest and remotest islands, within the last twenty or thirty years. Unemployment is virtually unknown, drudgery equally uncommon, and the result is an alive and contented community.

Now I have no intention of holding up Orkney as a model for imitation, or putting forward a programme of small holdings as a cure for the disastrous economic condition of society. The life on these little farms in the Orkneys is humanly desirable and good and fulfils all the claims that Mr. Belloc and Mr. Chesterton make for their theory of Distributism. But it is a life quite eccentric to the economic life of modern civilisation; an erratic fruition; an end; not a factor which can be taken into account in the painful and vital processes through which society is passing at present. I draw attention to it for quite a different reason: because it represented the only desirable form of life that I found in all my journey through Scotland. It has achieved this, one might almost say, by a happy series of drawbacks, or what seem at first sight to be drawbacks: by its isolation for centuries from the rest of Scotland and Great Britain, an isolation which has enabled it to preserve its traditional ways of life, so that until to-day it has scarcely been touched by the competitive spirit of Industrialism, and has remained largely co-operative; and by the fact that it has at the same time been able to take advantage of scientific discoveries which are a specific product of Industrialism. It has managed, as far as that is humanly possible, to have its cake and eat it. It has been saved by being just outside the circumference of the industrial world, near enough to know about it, but too far off to be drawn into it. Now it seems to me that this is the only way in which any community can achieve a partial salvation to-day and live a desirable life, surrounded by an industrial world. There are people who think that a whole nation can live in the midst of industrial capitalism as if they were separated from it: people such as the Hitlerites in Germany, who in industrial conditions expect the population to practise the traditional peasant virtues. I suspect that at the back of the Scottish Nationalist movement there is also some such expectation; if there is, it is certainly futile; for traditional virtues take a long time to mature, and cannot be created by a mere desire that they should exist but only by the specific conditions that naturally produce them. This is a lesson which the Orkney Islands teach with quite peculiar force. Certain conditions, aided by human intelligence, have there, after centuries of hardship, produced something which is natural and inevitable and at the same time humanly desirable. The hope for industrial society is that it, too, will eventually develop in this way; but the result will certainly be very different from the Orkney Islands.

CHAPTER VI

CONCLUSION

WHEN one comes to the end of a journey one feels a desire to turn back and cast a last glance over all the impressions one has gathered, even though they should be as casual as a collection of shells picked up on a sea-shore. Scotland itself could only be known by someone who had the power to live simultaneously in the bodies of all the men, women and children in it. I took a chance cut through it, stopping here and there, picking up this or that object, gathering shells whose meaning was often obscure or illegible to me. I did not find anything which I could call Scotland; anything, that is to say, beyond the vague and wandering image already impressed upon me by memory: the net result of my having been brought up in it, and of living in it until I was nearly thirty, and lastly of belonging to it.

My deepest impression, as I have said already, was one of emptiness, and that applied even more to the towns than to the country-side. Scotland is losing its industries, as it lost a hundred years ago a great deal of its agriculture and most of its indigenous literature. The waste glens of Sutherlandshire and the literary depopulation of Edinburgh and Glasgow were not

obvious blows at Scotland's existence, and so they were
accepted without serious protest, for the general
absorption in industrial progress and money blinded
everybody to them. Now Scotland's industry, like its
intelligence before it, is gravitating to England, but its
population is sitting where it did before, in the company of disused coal-pits and silent ship-yards.

It may be objected that in England, too, there are a
great number of people in the same plight; but the
state of things in Scotland is much worse, as is shown
by the unemployment figures, and it is continuing to
grow worse. The following facts from an excellent
article which appeared in the *Sunday Referee* of
March 3rd, 1935, give a good idea of the comparative
states of the two countries. "It is not generally realised
that the depression has followed a different course in
Scotland and in England in two particulars. It has
been markedly more severe in Scotland, and Scotland
has shown much less elasticity in recovery.

"As to relative severity, the unemployment figures
speak for themselves. In July, 1933, when things were
at about their worst, the percentages of insured persons out of employment were as follows: Wales, 33
per cent; Scotland, 28 per cent; England, including
Wales, 16 per cent.

"The worst single area in England proper, the
North, stood at 21.29 per cent. Clearly the high Welsh
figure contributed to sending the English figure up to
16 per cent.

"It seems reasonable to suggest that unemployment

in England alone stood at about 14 per cent. or half the percentage of Scotland.

"Moreover, unemployment figures have come down far more rapidly in England than in Scotland, and, indeed, in Scotland the tendency is once more towards a rise.

"In the primary industrial areas, where the conditions are similar to those of industrial Scotland, about 55,000 have gone back to work in the past three months. A similar improvement in Scotland would have involved rather more than 7,000 persons. Actually, Scottish unemployment has gone up by 15,262."

The author of the article attributes a great deal of the blame for this state of things to rationalisation. "In practice both the Government and the private industrial combines have shown a tendency to axe Scottish concerns before English ones." The Government axed Rosyth. "Railway amalgamation has meant the axing of Scottish locomotive building works at Perth, Inverness, and Inverurie, and a great reduction in the work done in Glasgow. In Inverness the number of railway employees fell from 1,000 to 50. Further, these Scottish works were replaced by new works erected in England, so that railway amalgamation has decreased unemployment in England at the price of increasing it in Scotland. Similar tales could be told of textiles, shipbuilding, ironworks, sugar-refining, and chemical works." Also it should be added that while many new secondary industries have sprung up in England during the past few years, swelling the volume of wealth and employment, there is virtually no sign of them in Scotland.

There are two ways of facing these disastrous facts. One is Nationalism. Industry is leaving Scotland and going to England: therefore, the Nationalists argue, the partnership of the two countries is a bad one for Scotland, and it could do better if left to itself. Moreover, the union of the banks some years ago established the control of Great Britain's credit in London; and the investor is more willing to put his money into an industry that is near at hand and that he can keep his eye upon than in some concern at the other end of the island. The Scottish Nationalists maintain that if they had a Scottish Government with a financial organ of its own they could put an end to this anomaly and make Scottish industry as prosperous as English. There is nothing to prevent this, they hold, but the Union and the Bank of England.

This is a perfectly reasonable argument within the present system. If the Nationalists' ideas were put into practice it would no doubt help to redress the inequality between the two countries: the unemployed figures in Scotland would probably decrease, and those of England simultaneously go up; that is, assuming that the present industrial system continued. There would still be a fairly big residue of unemployment; the slums would still exist as they are; the great majority of the people would still be poor; the workman would still live in fear of being thrown out of his job. In return the population would have the comfort of knowing they were citizens of an independent Scotland, of being poor on Scottish notes and coins instead of on English, of drawing the dole from a Scottish Government instead of the present one, and of being examined on Dunbar and Burns in the schools in place of Shakespeare and Milton. That would no doubt be better than the present state of things, but it does not seem to me an end worth striving very hard for. Nationalists may say that I am misrepresenting them, and that if they succeed in making Scotland a nation they will put an end to unemployment and poverty. But if that is so, they should say so quite clearly now, so that everybody might know; and they should also say by what means they intend to achieve this. Instead they have decided to widen the basis of their appeal so as to attract people of every shade of political opinion, Conservative, Liberal, Labour, and Socialist. This has put them in the absurd position of being unable to make any pronouncement on the one question which most concerns everybody to-day, not only in Scotland, but in the whole civilised world— the economic question. They dare not make a statement of any colour on it, lest they should scare away prospective Conservative or Liberal or Socialist members of the party. That, even from the Nationalist point of view, is surely a bad policy. A movement does not grow by being generally inoffensive, but by setting before it an aim important and definite enough to attract to it an increasing number of supporters.

The conclusion that I came to after seeing what I saw of Scotland was that the fundamental cause of its many ills, including even the de-nationalisation of its people, was economic and not national. The withdrawal of industry from Scotland to England is the result of an economic process, for which there is one explanation in Marx and another in the theories of Major Douglas; and it would have happened just as certainly if Scotland had been an English county. It has happened because Scotland is at the circumference of the economic circle whose centre is London, not because Scotland is inhabited by a race foreign to the English. The upper middle classes of Scotland, again, are being Anglicised not because they prefer England to their own country, but because an English accent and English manners are of more economic and social value in present-day society than a Scottish accent and Scottish manners. The Scottish proletariat have been de-nationalised not by English influence or English rule, but by the operation of an industrial system conducted on a basis of individualism. The break-down of the old democratic forms of Scottish life has been brought about by the great contrasts of wealth and poverty produced by that system, not by the influence of the English aristocratic ideal, which in any case is virtually dead. The same power has dried up the life of the small country towns and turned them into places like Thrums. Had Scotland never ceased to be an independent nation, most of these changes, including a great measure of de-nationalisation, would have happened, for they are the results of a general process which no national frontiers could have shut out. But if that is so, then it is clear that the regeneration of Scotland can only be brought about by an economic change, and that the Nationalist movement is at most a symptom or a by-product of historical conditions, not a genuine factor in them. After my stay in Glasgow, indeed, I never doubted that.

I can imagine Scotland freed from Capitalism and using all its rich resources for the good of all its people. A Scotland which achieved that end would be a nation, but it would not care very much whether it was called a nation or not: the problem would have become an academic one. On the other hand, the Scottish qualities which the Nationalists wish to revive artificially would then probably revive of themselves, since the system that has helped most to destroy them would no longer exist. The divisions of race and culture which at present cause so much friction, the division between the Highlands and the Lowlands and between both and the large Irish population, would simply not matter any longer, for it is competition in the labour market which has caused almost all the trouble between these races. One can imagine a nation living in comfort and freedom; supporting a numerous peasantry on wide tracts that are waste now; Glasgow a new and handsome city; the industries carried on with decency and order; Edinburgh a centre for the arts; in short, a country which would be a harmoniously working and interdependent unity from the Borders to the Shetland

Islands. That end is far away; but it is far away not because it could not be realised with the present machinery of production, but because the people, in Scotland as in other countries, are blind to their own good and divided among themselves. There is no doubt that the Scottish people, with their immense store of potential energy, would be capable of using the resources of modern production to create a society such as I have imagined. An enormous change must happen before that can take place, it is true; but the development of Industrialism itself is driving us towards such a change. The only political question of any importance now is how that development is to be directed, how the transition is to be made. That question is an economic, not a national question. One cannot imagine that the change can be made easily, that is, without the exercise either of hard thought or of senseless violence, and the first is the only thing that can save us from the second; but one can just as little imagine that it will never be made at all. Scotland, with its derelict industries, its vast slums, its depopulated glens, its sweated peasantry, and its army of unemployed, has no future save through such a change. This view may seem at first a depressing one; but to me it seems the only cheerful one.